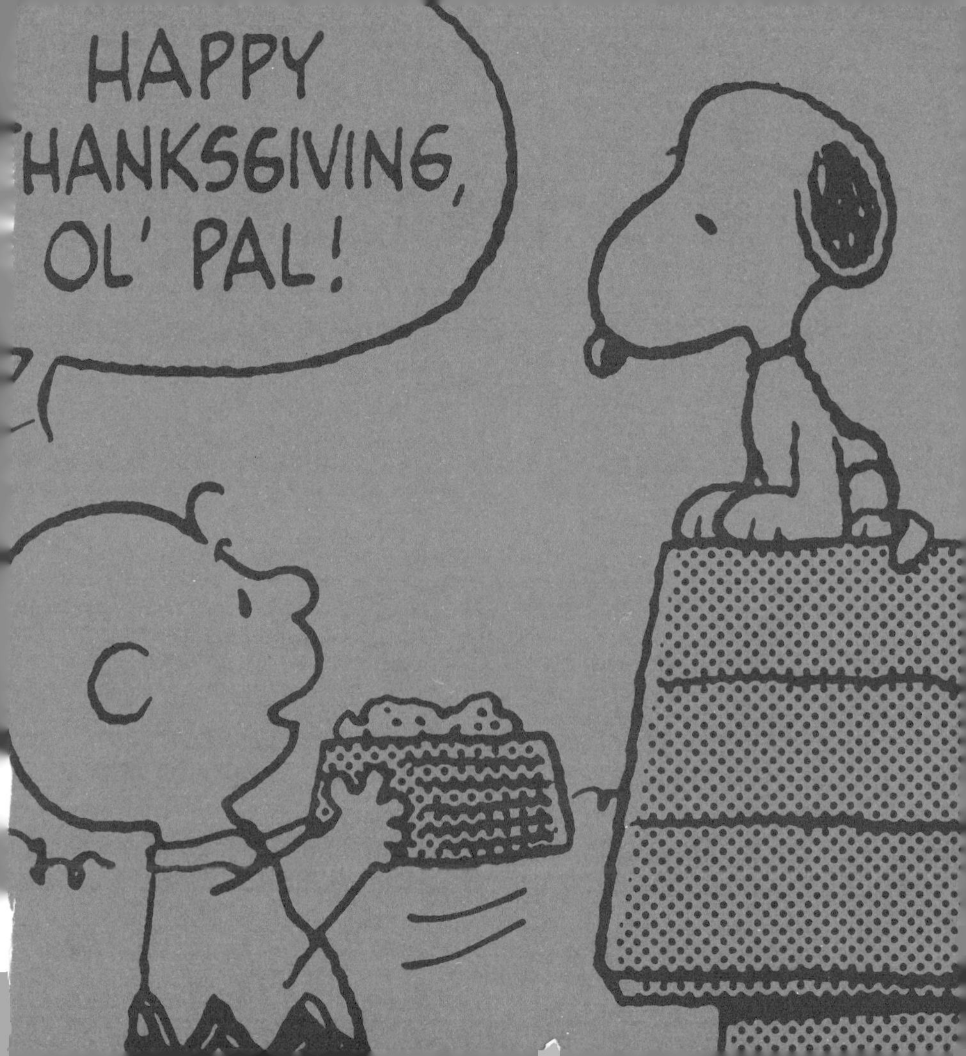
HAPPY THANKSGIVING, OL' PAL!

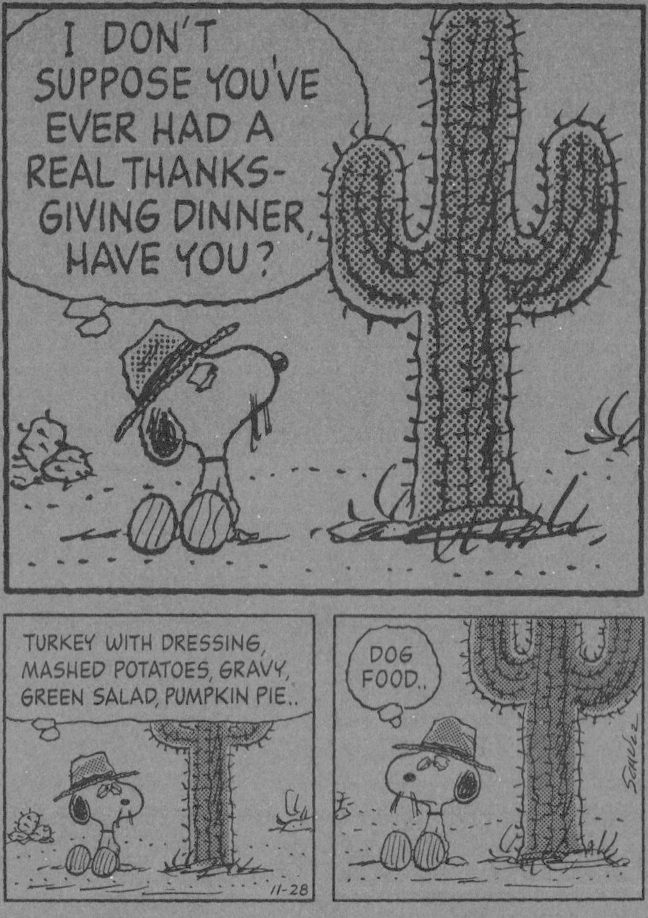
I DON'T SUPPOSE YOU'VE EVER HAD A REAL THANKS-GIVING DINNER, HAVE YOU?
TURKEY WITH DRESSING, MASHED POTATOES, GRAVY, GREEN SALAD, PUMPKIN PIE..
11-28
DOG FOOD..
SCHULZ

Snoopy's Thanksgiving

CHARLES M. SCHULZ

FANTAGRAPHICS BOOKS, SEATTLE

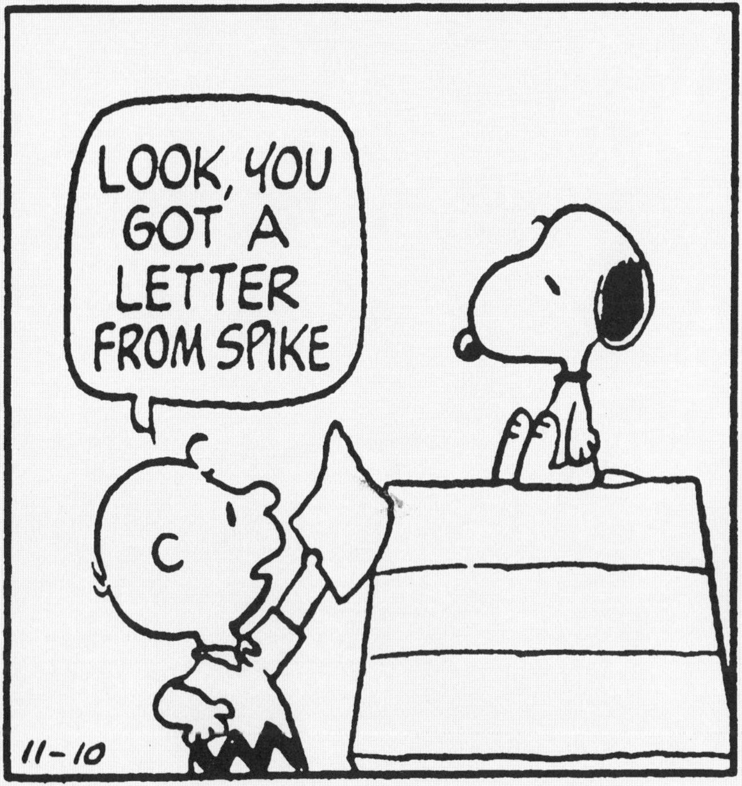
LOOK, YOU GOT A LETTER FROM SPIKE
11-10

"SNOOPY'S THANKSGIVING INVITATION"

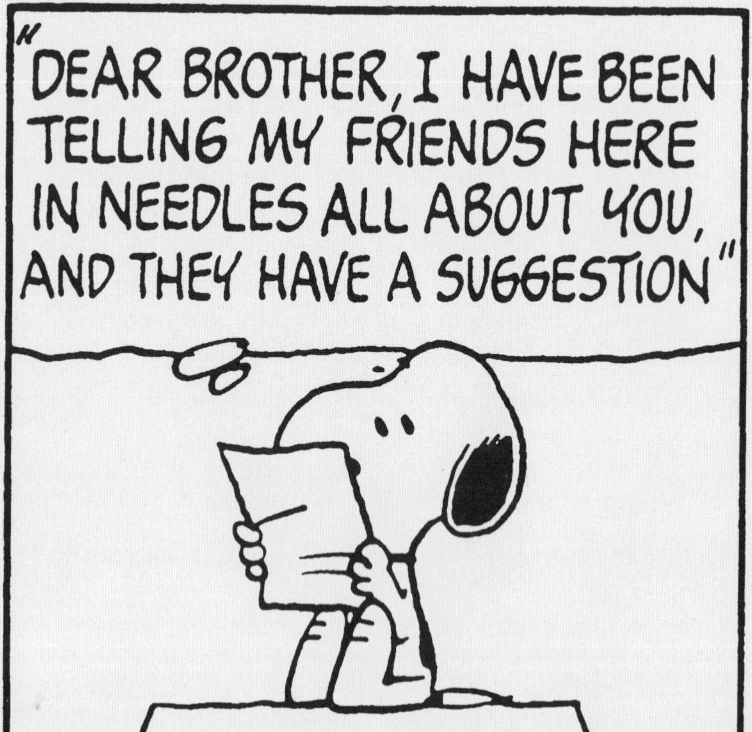
"DEAR BROTHER, I HAVE BEEN TELLING MY FRIENDS HERE IN NEEDLES ALL ABOUT YOU, AND THEY HAVE A SUGGESTION"

"SNOOPY'S THANKSGIVING INVITATION"

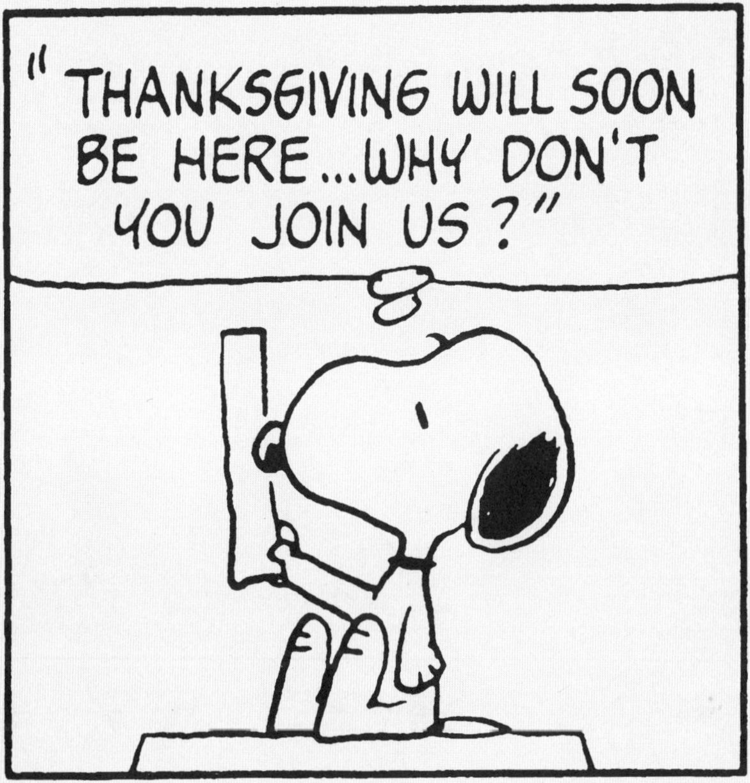
"THANKSGIVING WILL SOON BE HERE...WHY DON'T YOU JOIN US?"

"SNOOPY'S THANKSGIVING INVITATION"

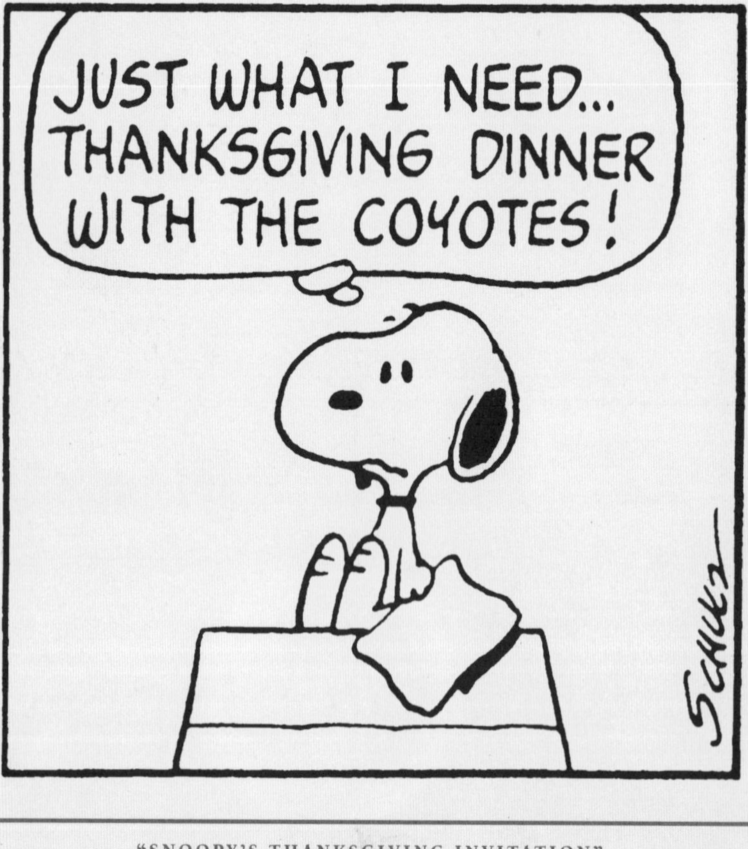
JUST WHAT I NEED... THANKSGIVING DINNER WITH THE COYOTES!
SCHULZ

"SNOOPY'S THANKSGIVING INVITATION"

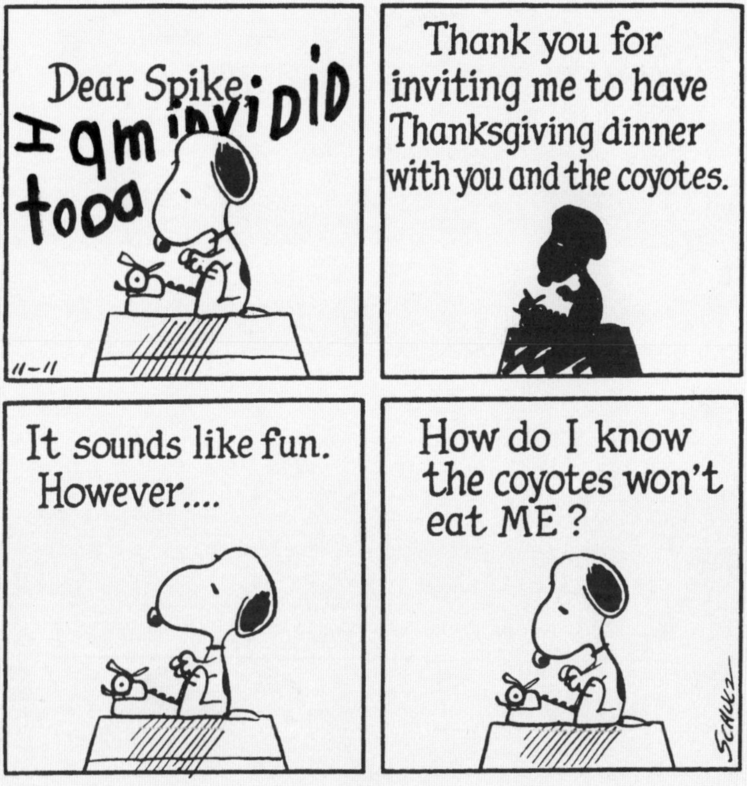
Dear Spike:
11-11
Thank you for inviting me to have Thanksgiving dinner with you and the coyotes.
It sounds like fun. However....
How do I know the coyotes won't eat ME ?
SCHULZ

"SNOOPY'S THANKSGIVING INVITATION"

HERE, YOU GOT ANOTHER LETTER FROM SPIKE...
11-12
"DEAR BROTHER, PLEASE TRY TO COME TO NEEDLES FOR THANKSGIVING"
"THERE'S A CUTE LITTLE COYOTE HERE WHO IS DYING TO MEET YOU... I'VE TOLD HER ALL ABOUT YOU"
I'LL GO!!
SCHULZ

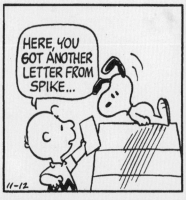

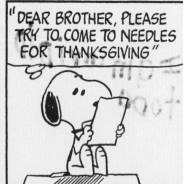

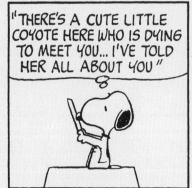

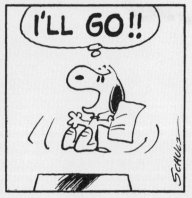

"SNOOPY'S THANKSGIVING INVITATION"

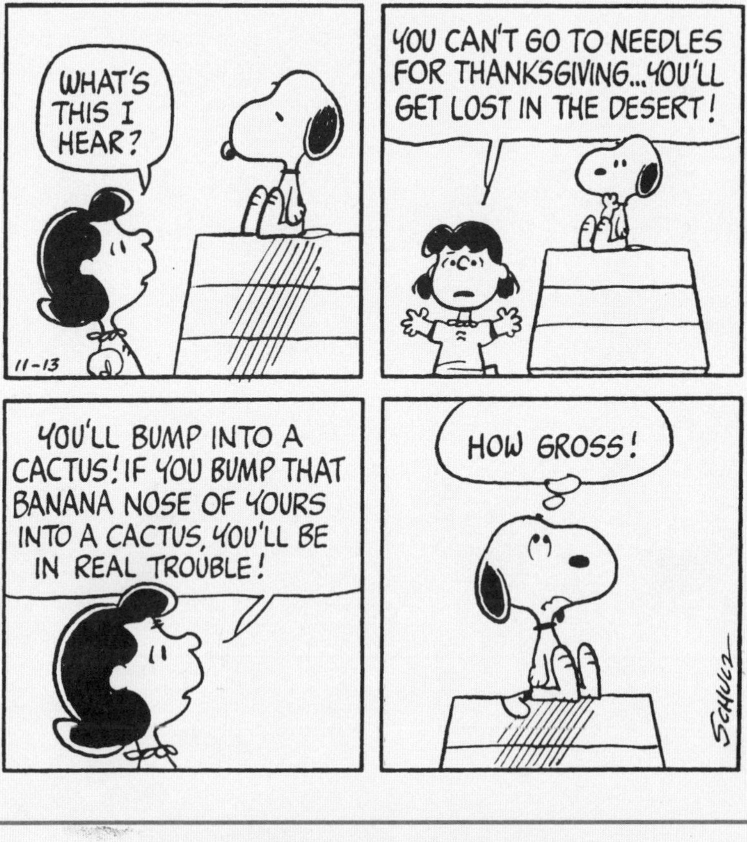
WHAT'S THIS I HEAR?
11-13
YOU CAN'T GO TO NEEDLES FOR THANKSGIVING...YOU'LL GET LOST IN THE DESERT!
YOU'LL BUMP INTO A CACTUS! IF YOU BUMP THAT BANANA NOSE OF YOURS INTO A CACTUS, YOU'LL BE IN REAL TROUBLE!
HOW GROSS!
SCHULZ

"SNOOPY'S THANKSGIVING INVITATION"

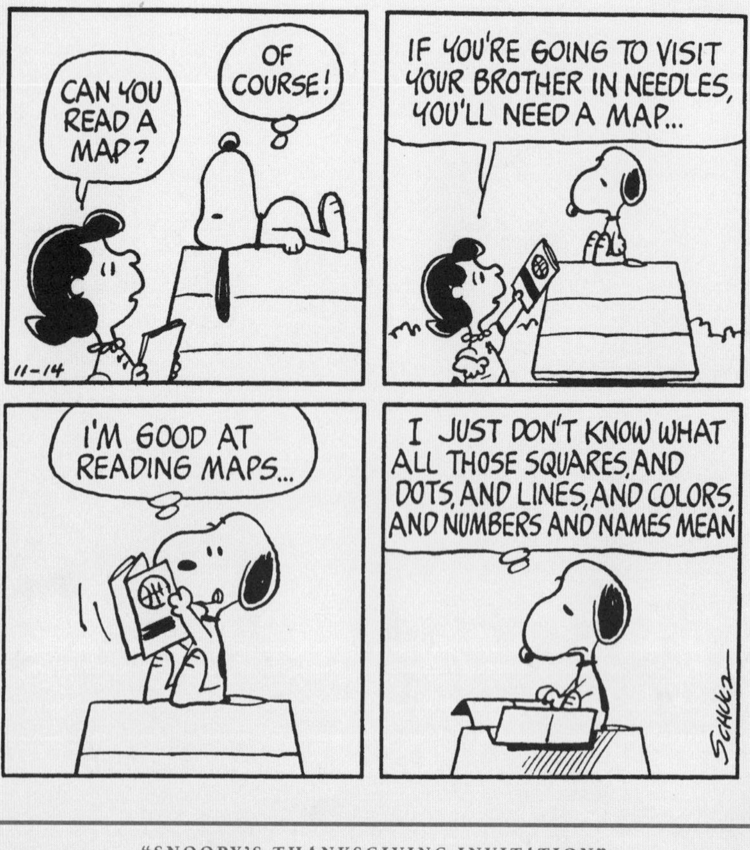
CAN YOU READ A MAP?
OF COURSE!
11-14
IF YOU'RE GOING TO VISIT YOUR BROTHER IN NEEDLES, YOU'LL NEED A MAP...
I'M GOOD AT READING MAPS...
I JUST DON'T KNOW WHAT ALL THOSE SQUARES, AND DOTS, AND LINES, AND COLORS, AND NUMBERS AND NAMES MEAN
SCHULZ

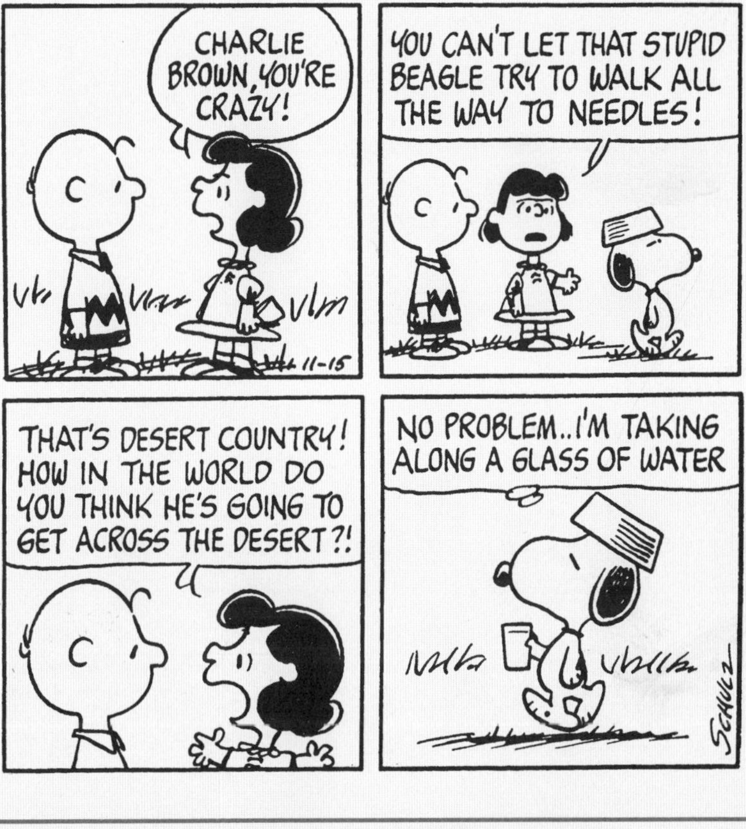
CHARLIE BROWN, YOU'RE CRAZY!
11-15
YOU CAN'T LET THAT STUPID BEAGLE TRY TO WALK ALL THE WAY TO NEEDLES!
THAT'S DESERT COUNTRY! HOW IN THE WORLD DO YOU THINK HE'S GOING TO GET ACROSS THE DESERT?!
NO PROBLEM..I'M TAKING ALONG A GLASS OF WATER
SCHULZ

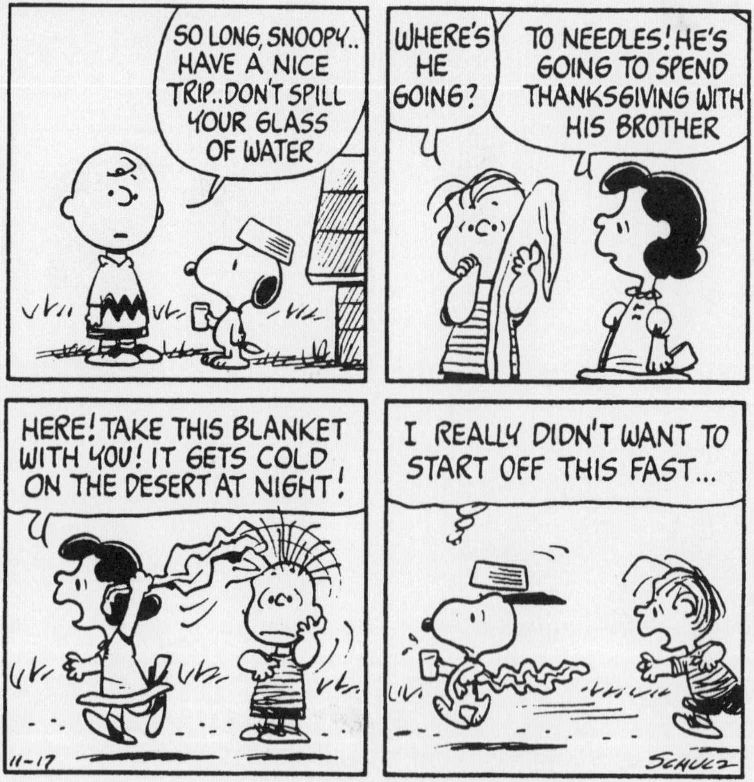
SO LONG, SNOOPY.. HAVE A NICE TRIP..DON'T SPILL YOUR GLASS OF WATER
WHERE'S HE GOING?
TO NEEDLES! HE'S GOING TO SPEND THANKSGIVING WITH HIS BROTHER
HERE! TAKE THIS BLANKET WITH YOU! IT GETS COLD ON THE DESERT AT NIGHT!
11-17
I REALLY DIDN'T WANT TO START OFF THIS FAST...
SCHULZ

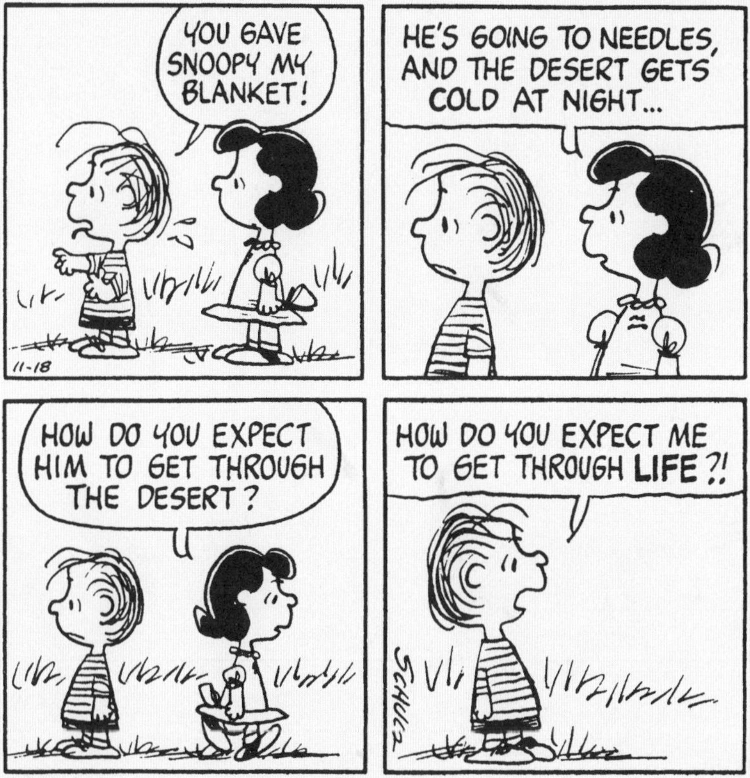
YOU GAVE SNOOPY MY BLANKET!
11-18
HE'S GOING TO NEEDLES, AND THE DESERT GETS COLD AT NIGHT...
HOW DO YOU EXPECT HIM TO GET THROUGH THE DESERT?
HOW DO YOU EXPECT ME TO GET THROUGH **LIFE**?!
SCHULZ

"SNOOPY'S THANKSGIVING INVITATION"

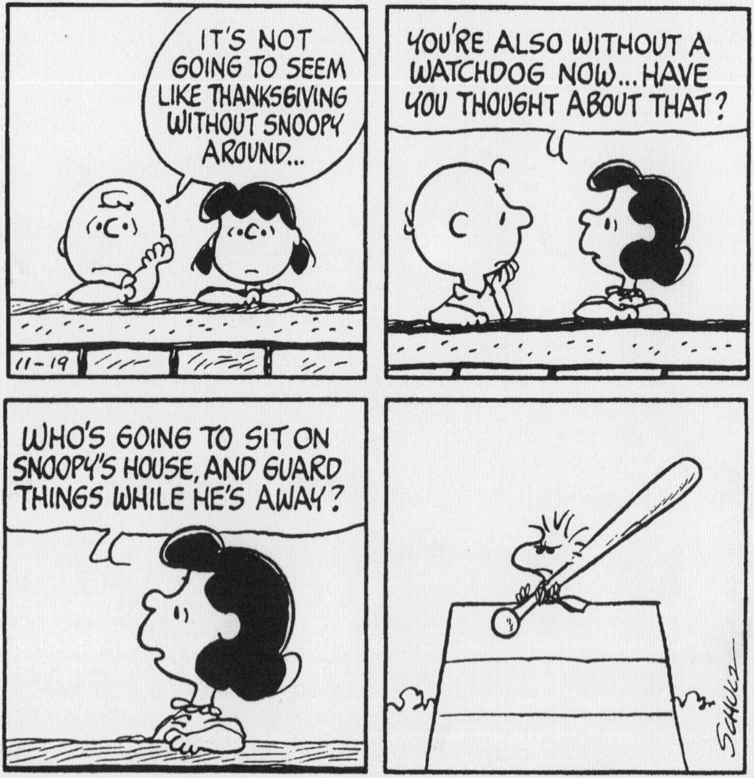
IT'S NOT GOING TO SEEM LIKE THANKSGIVING WITHOUT SNOOPY AROUND...
11-19
YOU'RE ALSO WITHOUT A WATCHDOG NOW... HAVE YOU THOUGHT ABOUT THAT?
WHO'S GOING TO SIT ON SNOOPY'S HOUSE, AND GUARD THINGS WHILE HE'S AWAY?
SCHULZ

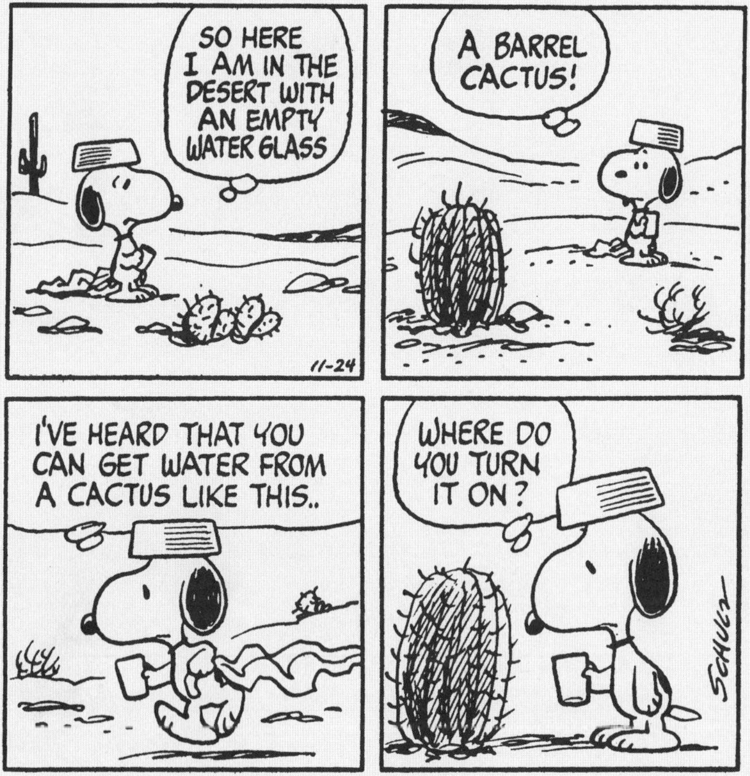
SO HERE I AM IN THE DESERT WITH AN EMPTY WATER GLASS
11-24
A BARREL CACTUS!
I'VE HEARD THAT YOU CAN GET WATER FROM A CACTUS LIKE THIS..
WHERE DO YOU TURN IT ON?
SCHULZ

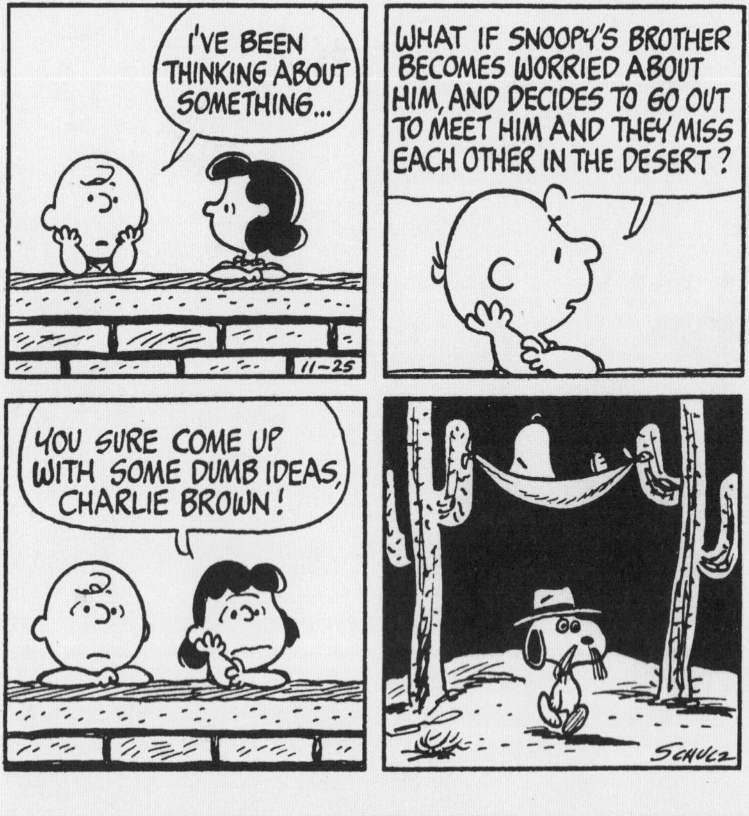
I'VE BEEN THINKING ABOUT SOMETHING...
WHAT IF SNOOPY'S BROTHER BECOMES WORRIED ABOUT HIM, AND DECIDES TO GO OUT TO MEET HIM AND THEY MISS EACH OTHER IN THE DESERT?
YOU SURE COME UP WITH SOME DUMB IDEAS, CHARLIE BROWN!
11-25
SCHULZ

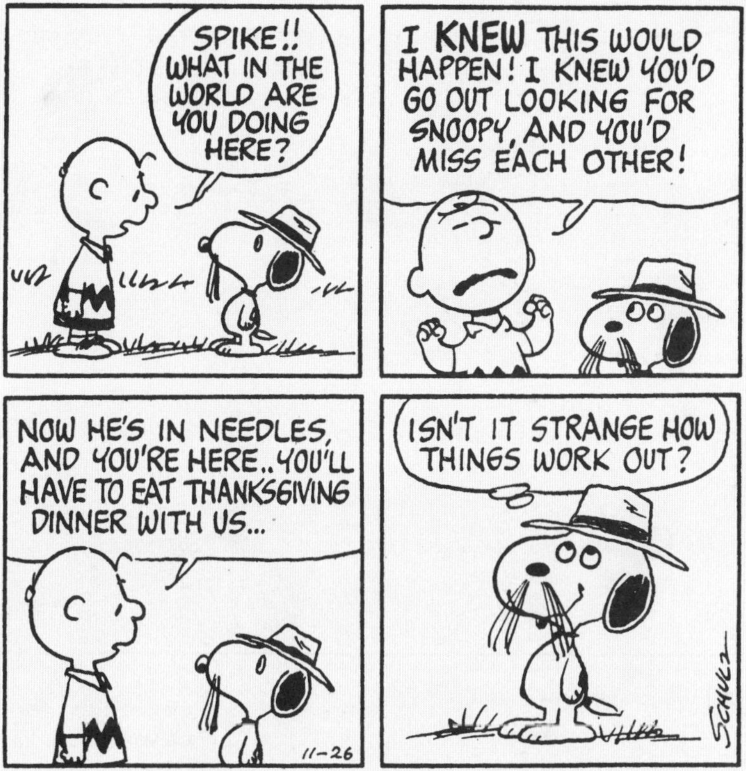
SPIKE!! WHAT IN THE WORLD ARE YOU DOING HERE?
I KNEW THIS WOULD HAPPEN! I KNEW YOU'D GO OUT LOOKING FOR SNOOPY, AND YOU'D MISS EACH OTHER!
NOW HE'S IN NEEDLES, AND YOU'RE HERE.. YOU'LL HAVE TO EAT THANKSGIVING DINNER WITH US...
11-26
ISN'T IT STRANGE HOW THINGS WORK OUT?
SCHULZ

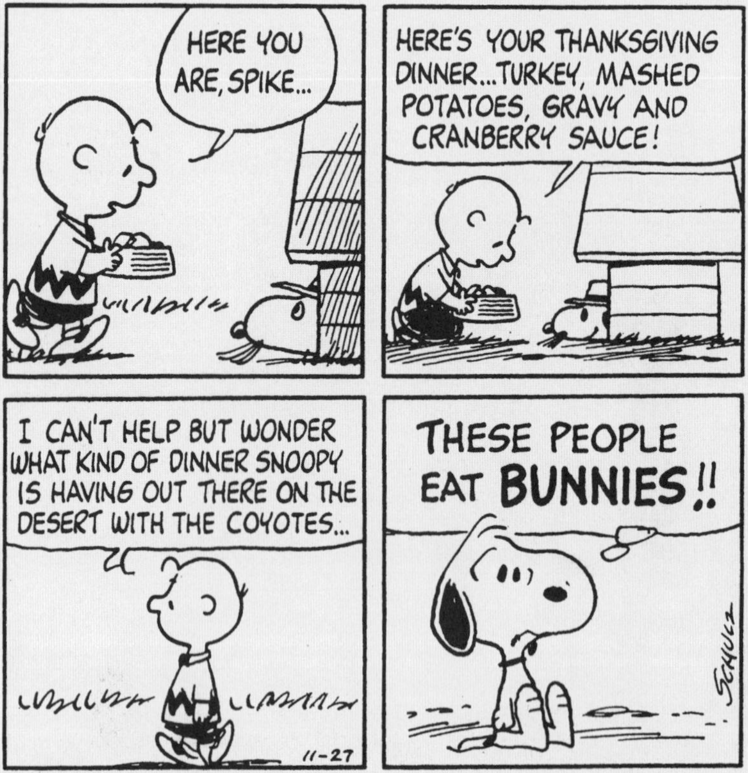
HERE YOU ARE, SPIKE...
HERE'S YOUR THANKSGIVING DINNER...TURKEY, MASHED POTATOES, GRAVY AND CRANBERRY SAUCE!
I CAN'T HELP BUT WONDER WHAT KIND OF DINNER SNOOPY IS HAVING OUT THERE ON THE DESERT WITH THE COYOTES...
11-27
THESE PEOPLE EAT BUNNIES!!
SCHULZ

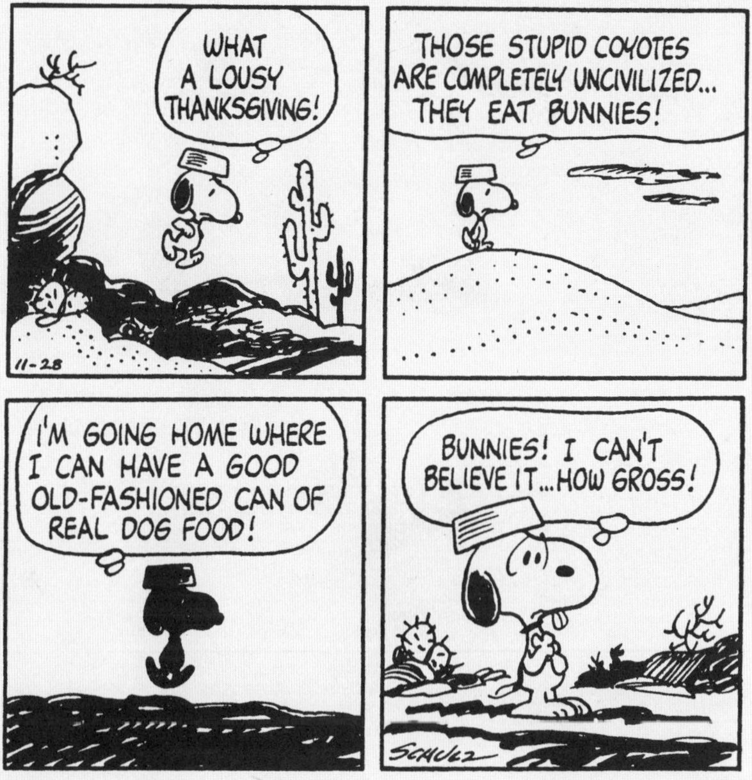
WHAT A LOUSY THANKSGIVING!
11-28
THOSE STUPID COYOTES ARE COMPLETELY UNCIVILIZED... THEY EAT BUNNIES!
I'M GOING HOME WHERE I CAN HAVE A GOOD OLD-FASHIONED CAN OF REAL DOG FOOD!
BUNNIES! I CAN'T BELIEVE IT...HOW GROSS!
SCHULZ

"SNOOPY'S THANKSGIVING INVITATION"

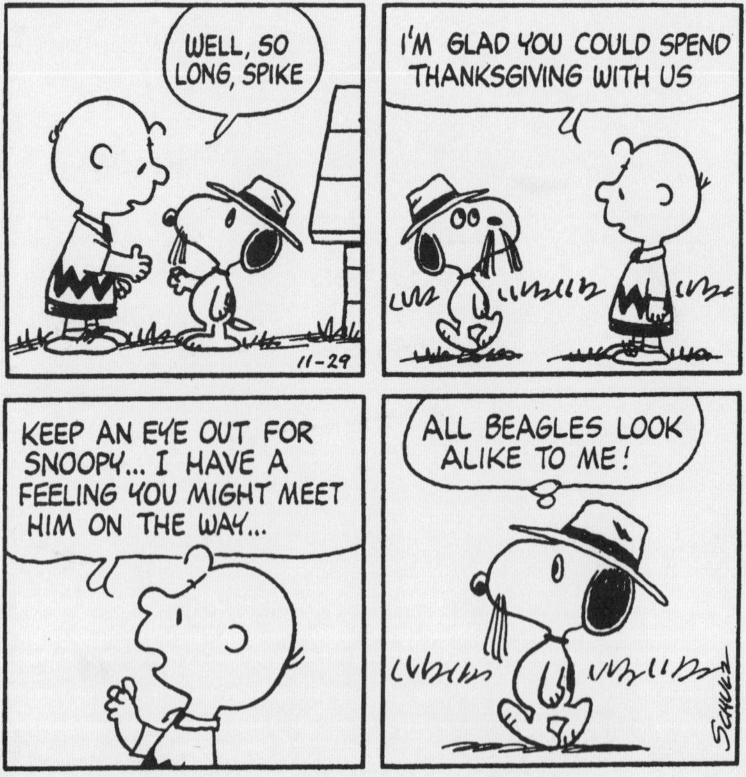
WELL, SO LONG, SPIKE
11-29
I'M GLAD YOU COULD SPEND THANKSGIVING WITH US
KEEP AN EYE OUT FOR SNOOPY... I HAVE A FEELING YOU MIGHT MEET HIM ON THE WAY...
ALL BEAGLES LOOK ALIKE TO ME!
SCHULZ

"SNOOPY'S THANKSGIVING INVITATION"

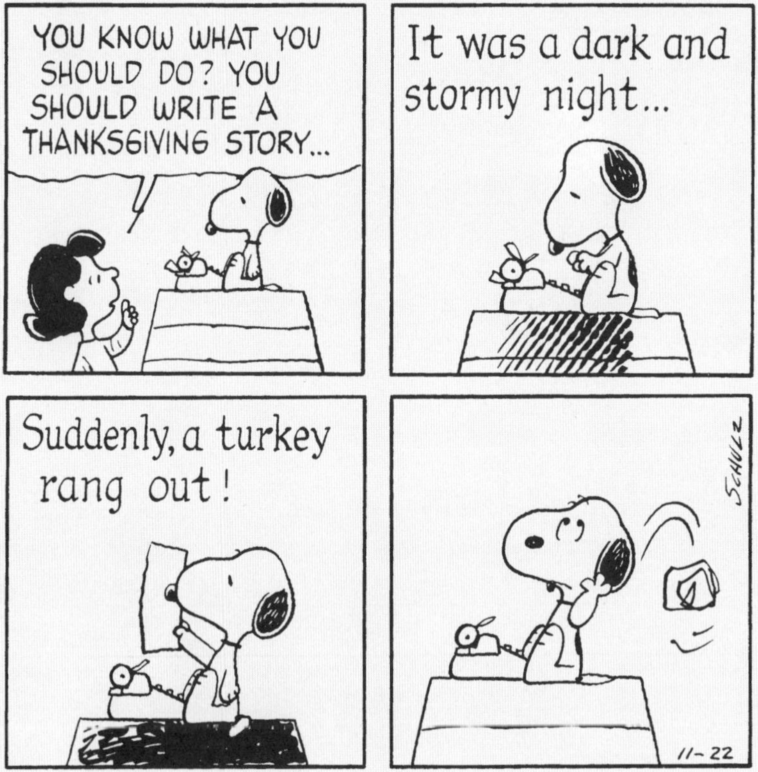
YOU KNOW WHAT YOU SHOULD DO? YOU SHOULD WRITE A THANKSGIVING STORY...
It was a dark and stormy night...
Suddenly, a turkey rang out!
SCHULZ
11-22

"LITERARY INSPIRATION"

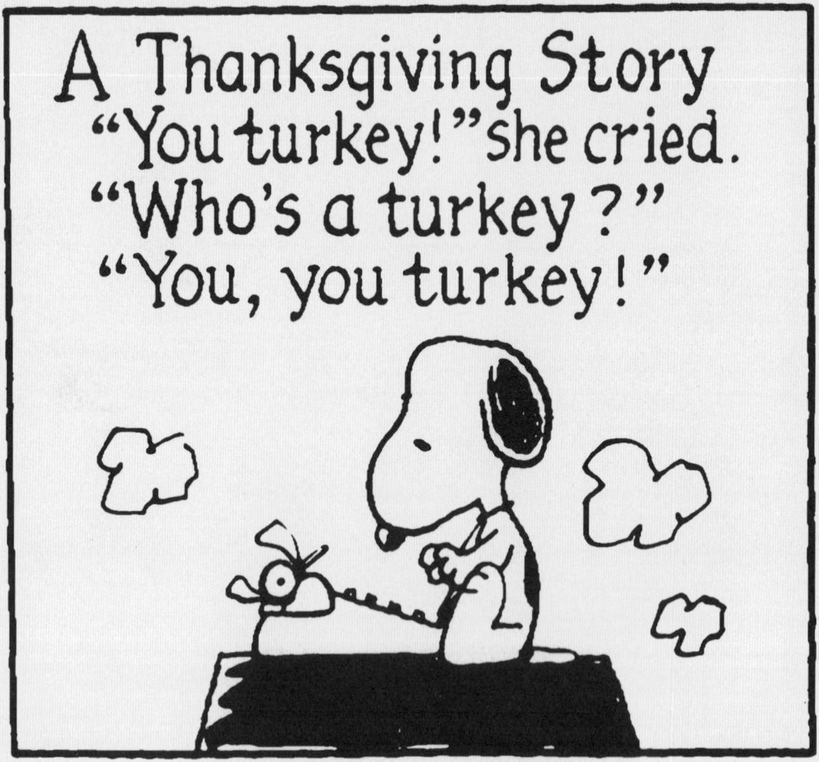

"LITERARY INSPIRATION"

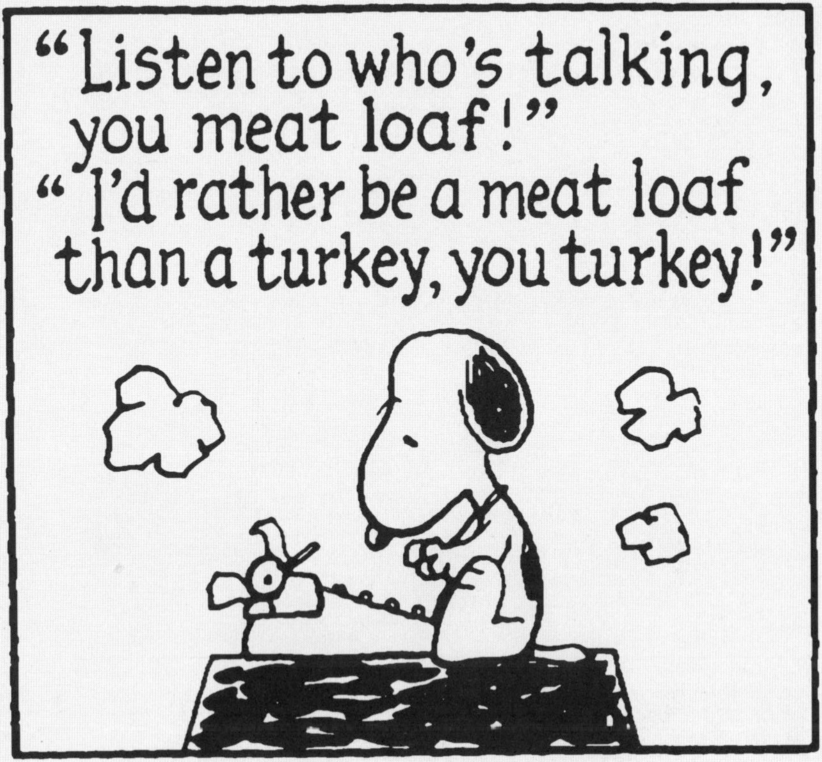

"LITERARY INSPIRATION"

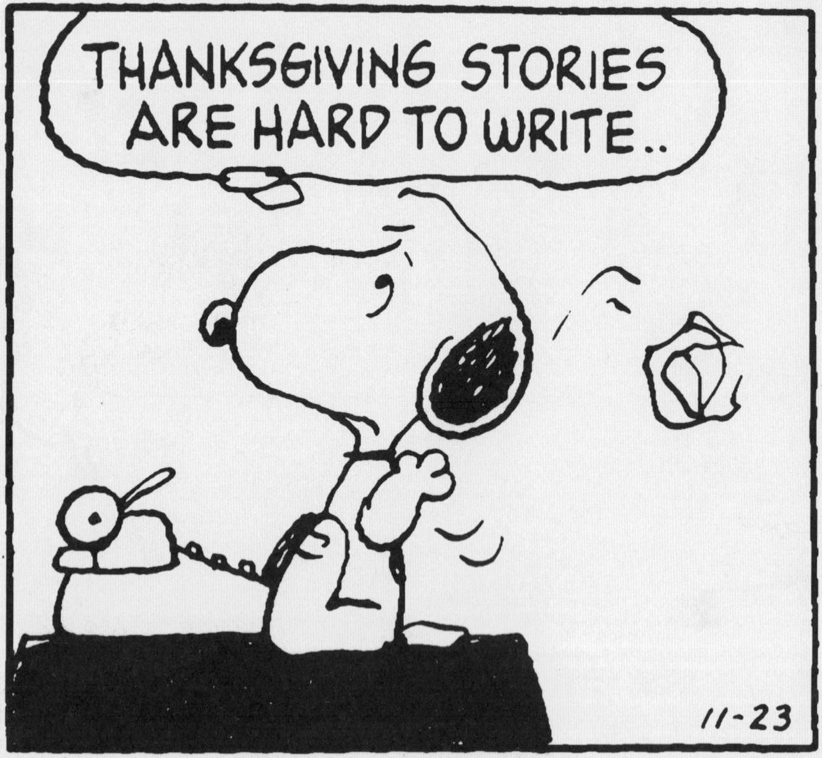
THANKSGIVING STORIES ARE HARD TO WRITE..
11-23

"LITERARY INSPIRATION"

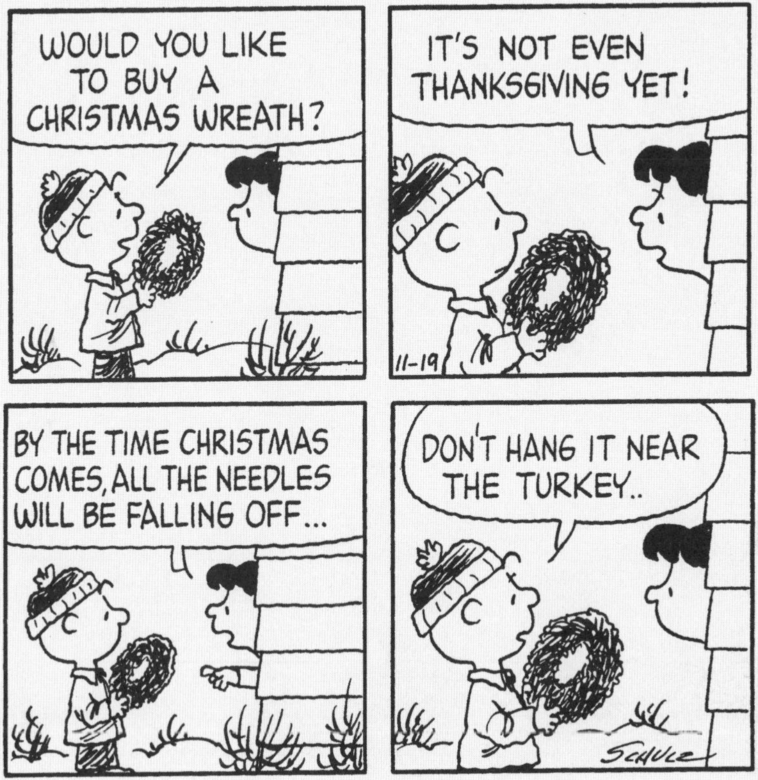
WOULD YOU LIKE TO BUY A CHRISTMAS WREATH?
IT'S NOT EVEN THANKSGIVING YET!
11-19
BY THE TIME CHRISTMAS COMES, ALL THE NEEDLES WILL BE FALLING OFF...
DON'T HANG IT NEAR THE TURKEY..
SCHULZ

"THANKSGIVING WREATH, PART I"

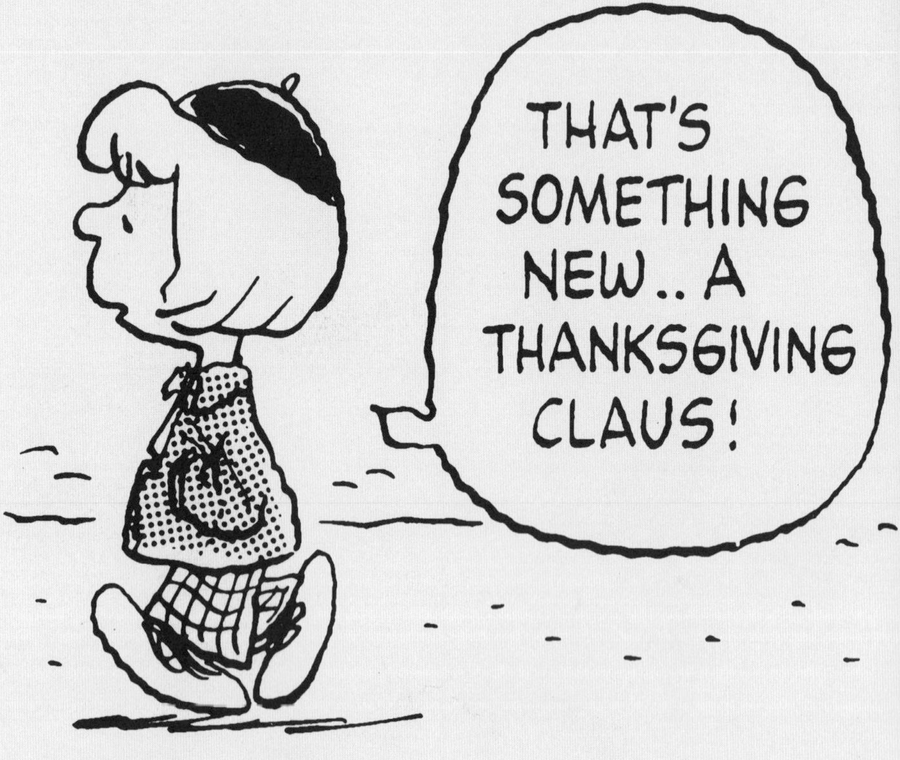
THAT'S SOMETHING NEW.. A THANKSGIVING CLAUS!

"THANKSGIVING CLAUS"

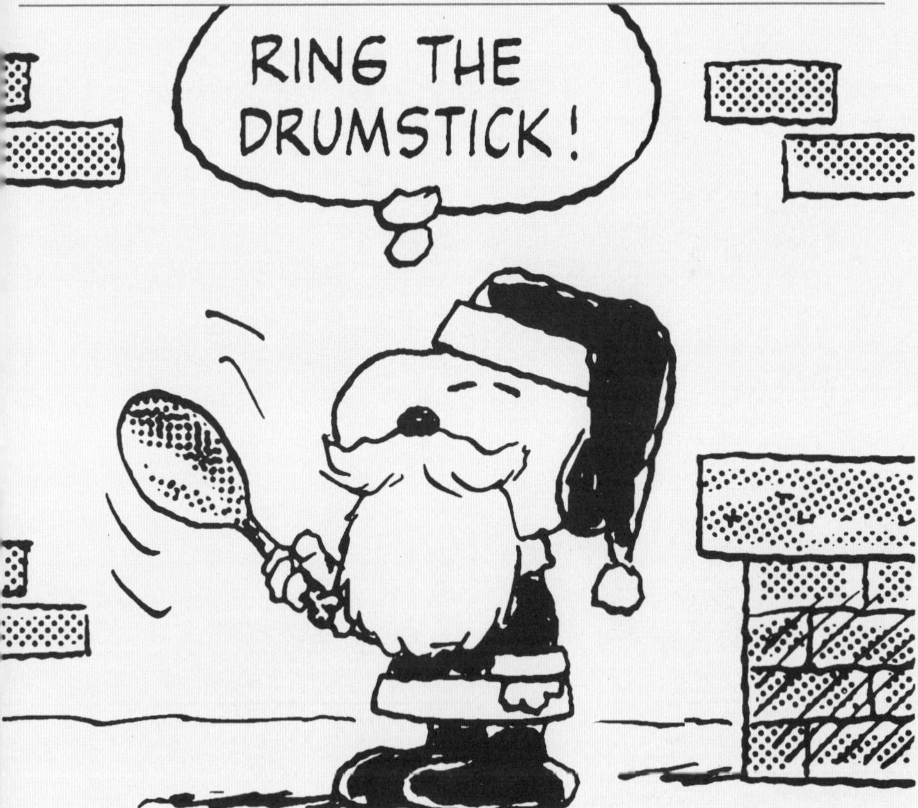
RING THE DRUMSTICK!

"THANKSGIVING CLAUS"

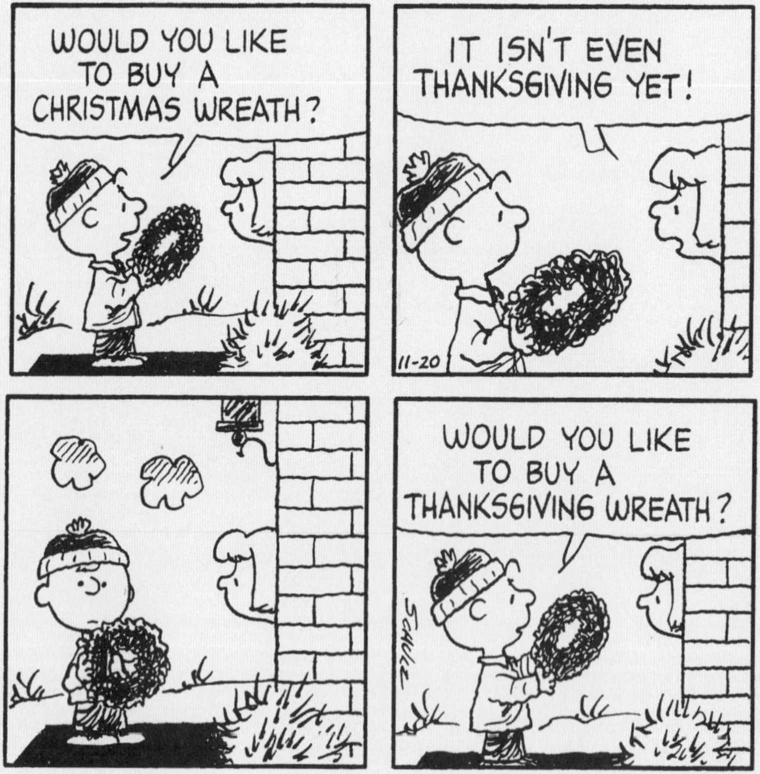
WOULD YOU LIKE TO BUY A CHRISTMAS WREATH?
IT ISN'T EVEN THANKSGIVING YET!
11-20
WOULD YOU LIKE TO BUY A THANKSGIVING WREATH?
SCHULZ

"THANKSGIVING WREATH, PART II"

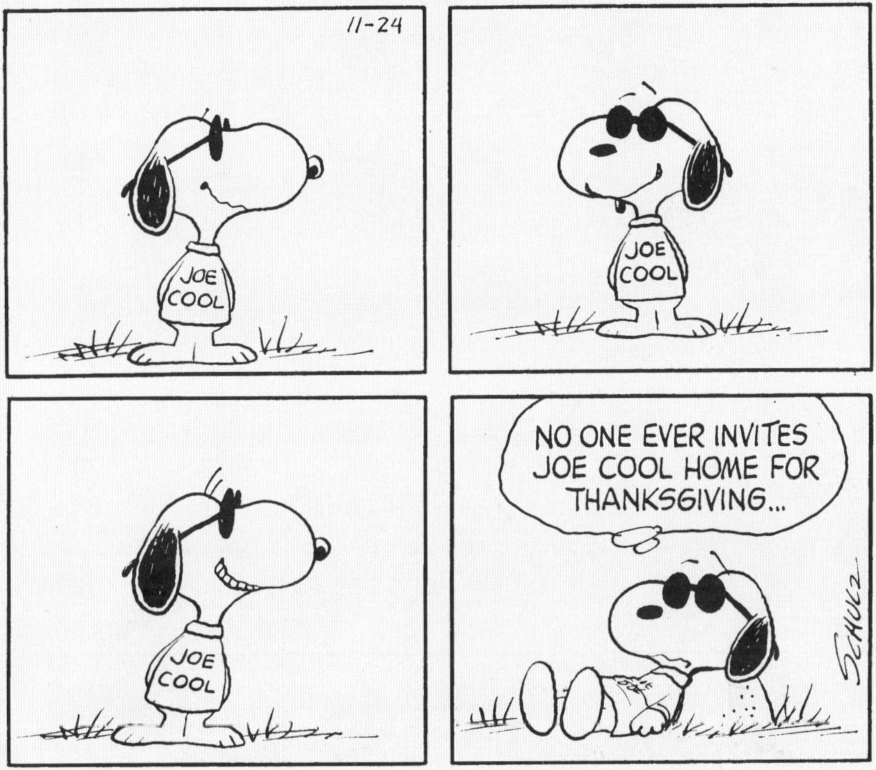
11-24
JOE COOL
JOE COOL
JOE COOL
NO ONE EVER INVITES JOE COOL HOME FOR THANKSGIVING...
SCHULZ

"JOE COOL'S THANKSGIVING"

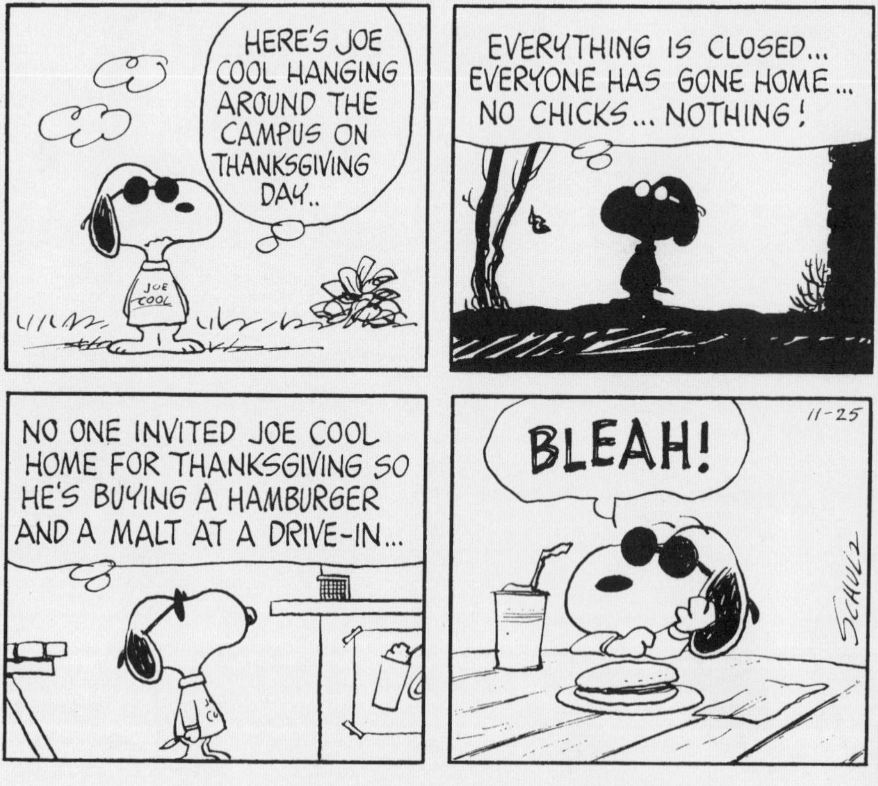
HERE'S JOE COOL HANGING AROUND THE CAMPUS ON THANKSGIVING DAY..
JOE COOL
EVERYTHING IS CLOSED... EVERYONE HAS GONE HOME... NO CHICKS... NOTHING!
NO ONE INVITED JOE COOL HOME FOR THANKSGIVING SO HE'S BUYING A HAMBURGER AND A MALT AT A DRIVE-IN...
11-25
BLEAH!
SCHULZ

"JOE COOL'S THANKSGIVING"

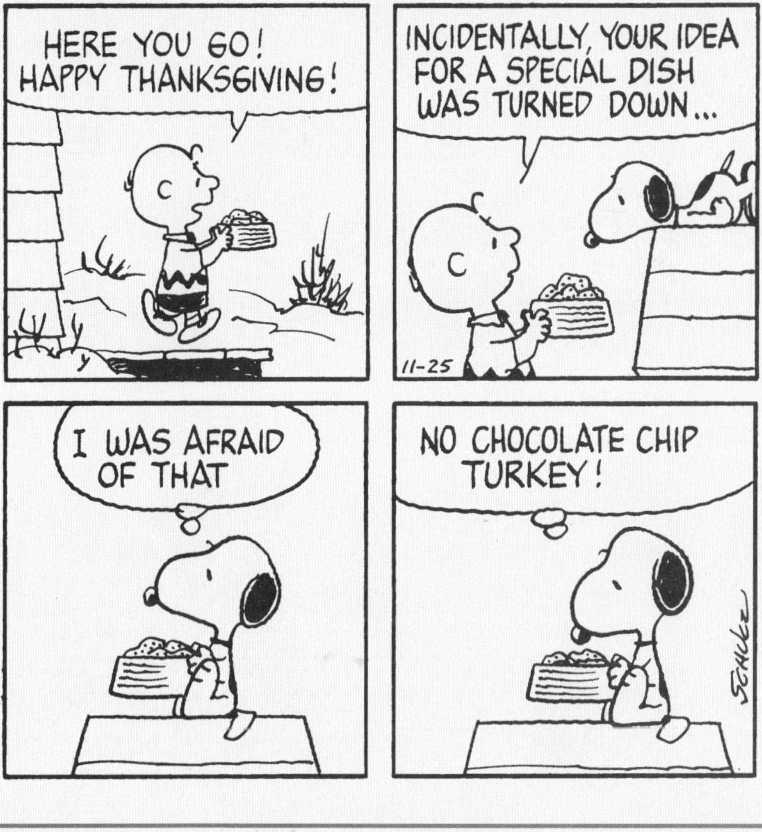
HERE YOU GO! HAPPY THANKSGIVING!
INCIDENTALLY, YOUR IDEA FOR A SPECIAL DISH WAS TURNED DOWN...
11-25
I WAS AFRAID OF THAT
NO CHOCOLATE CHIP TURKEY!
SCHULZ

"THANKSGIVING DINNER"

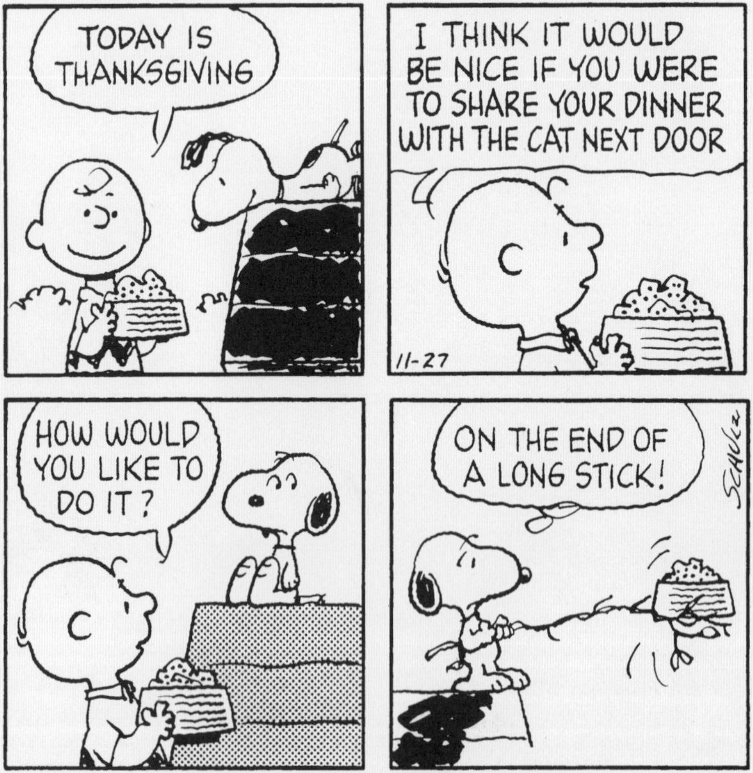
TODAY IS THANKSGIVING
I THINK IT WOULD BE NICE IF YOU WERE TO SHARE YOUR DINNER WITH THE CAT NEXT DOOR
11-27
HOW WOULD YOU LIKE TO DO IT ?
ON THE END OF A LONG STICK!
SCHULZ

"THANKSGIVING DINNER"

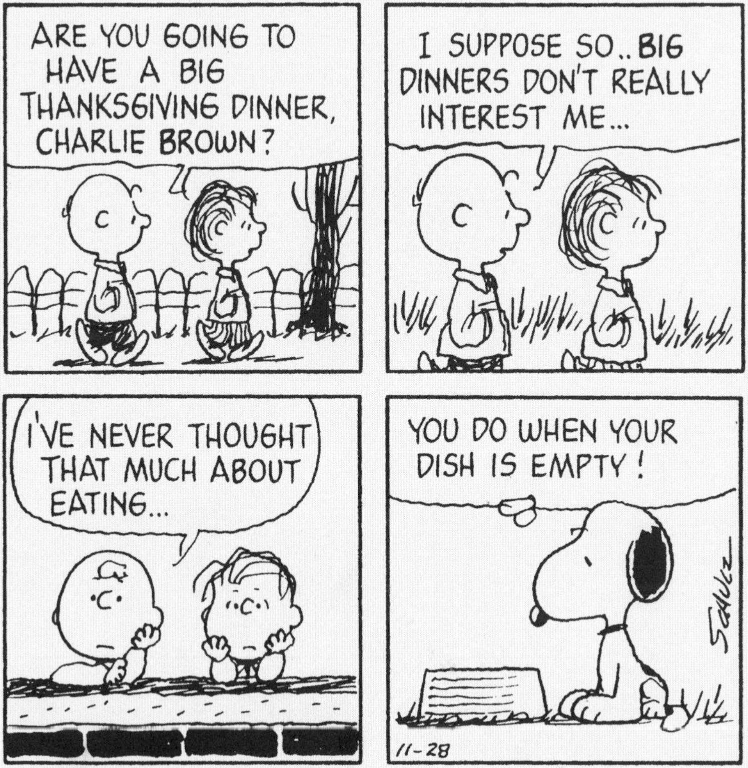
ARE YOU GOING TO HAVE A BIG THANKSGIVING DINNER, CHARLIE BROWN?
I SUPPOSE SO.. BIG DINNERS DON'T REALLY INTEREST ME...
I'VE NEVER THOUGHT THAT MUCH ABOUT EATING...
YOU DO WHEN YOUR DISH IS EMPTY!
SCHULZ
11-28

"THANKSGIVING DINNER"

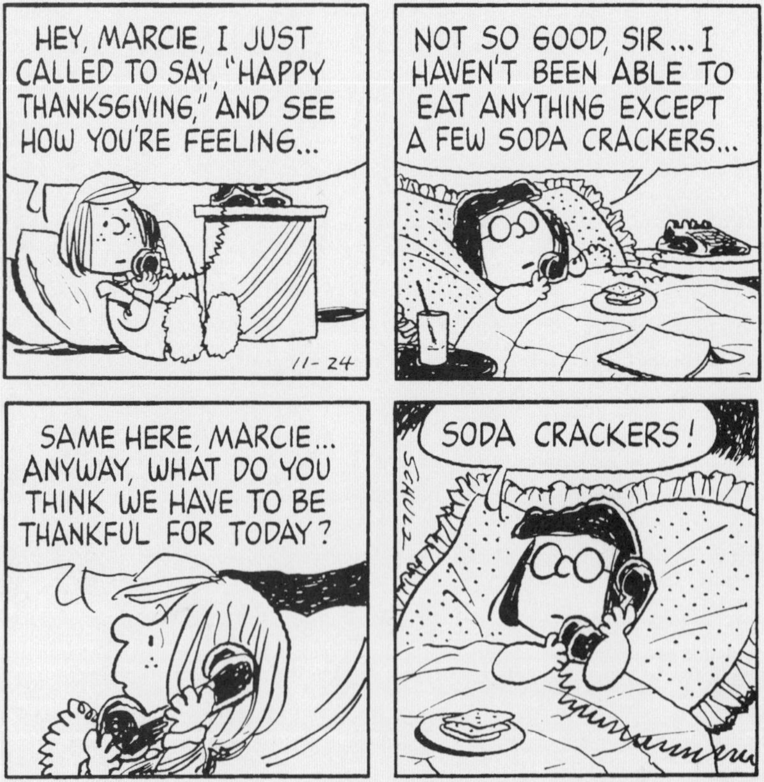
HEY, MARCIE, I JUST CALLED TO SAY, "HAPPY THANKSGIVING," AND SEE HOW YOU'RE FEELING...
11-24
NOT SO GOOD, SIR... I HAVEN'T BEEN ABLE TO EAT ANYTHING EXCEPT A FEW SODA CRACKERS...
SAME HERE, MARCIE... ANYWAY, WHAT DO YOU THINK WE HAVE TO BE THANKFUL FOR TODAY?
SCHULZ
SODA CRACKERS!

"THANKSGIVING DINNER"

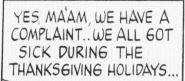

YES, MA'AM, WE HAVE A COMPLAINT.. WE ALL GOT SICK DURING THE THANKSGIVING HOLIDAYS...

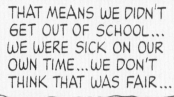

THAT MEANS WE DIDN'T GET OUT OF SCHOOL... WE WERE SICK ON OUR OWN TIME...WE DON'T THINK THAT WAS FAIR...

11-28

"GO SEE THE CHAPLAIN"?!

SARCASM DOES NOT BECOME YOU, MA'AM!

"THANKSGIVING DINNER"

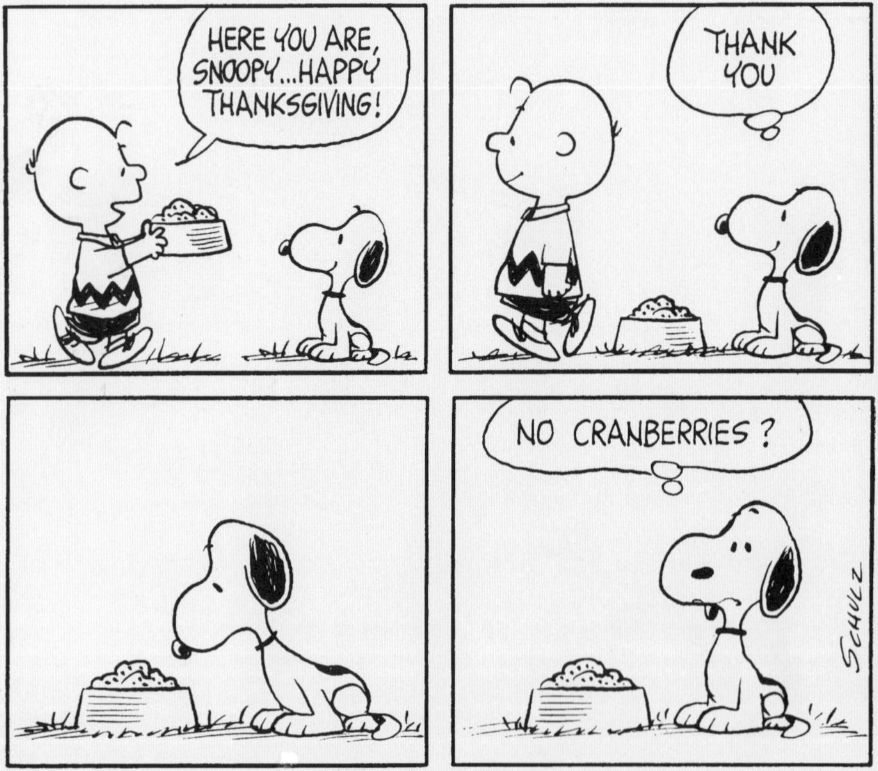
HERE YOU ARE, SNOOPY...HAPPY THANKSGIVING!
THANK YOU
NO CRANBERRIES ?
SCHULZ

"THANKSGIVING DINNER"

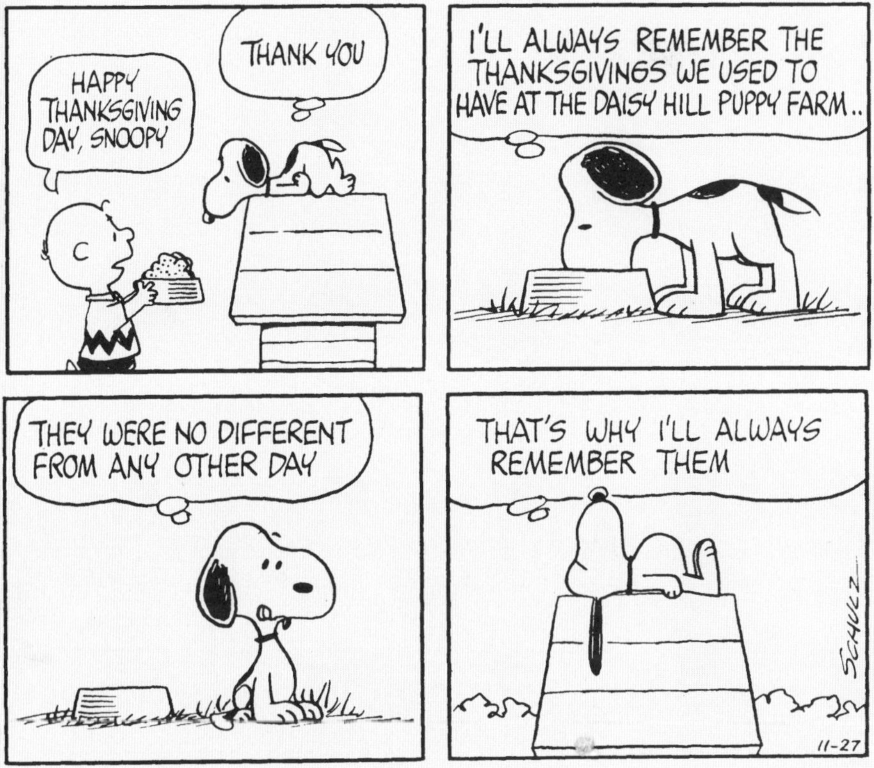
HAPPY THANKSGIVING DAY, SNOOPY
THANK YOU
I'LL ALWAYS REMEMBER THE THANKSGIVINGS WE USED TO HAVE AT THE DAISY HILL PUPPY FARM..
THEY WERE NO DIFFERENT FROM ANY OTHER DAY
THAT'S WHY I'LL ALWAYS REMEMBER THEM
SCHULZ
11-27

"THANKSGIVING DINNER"

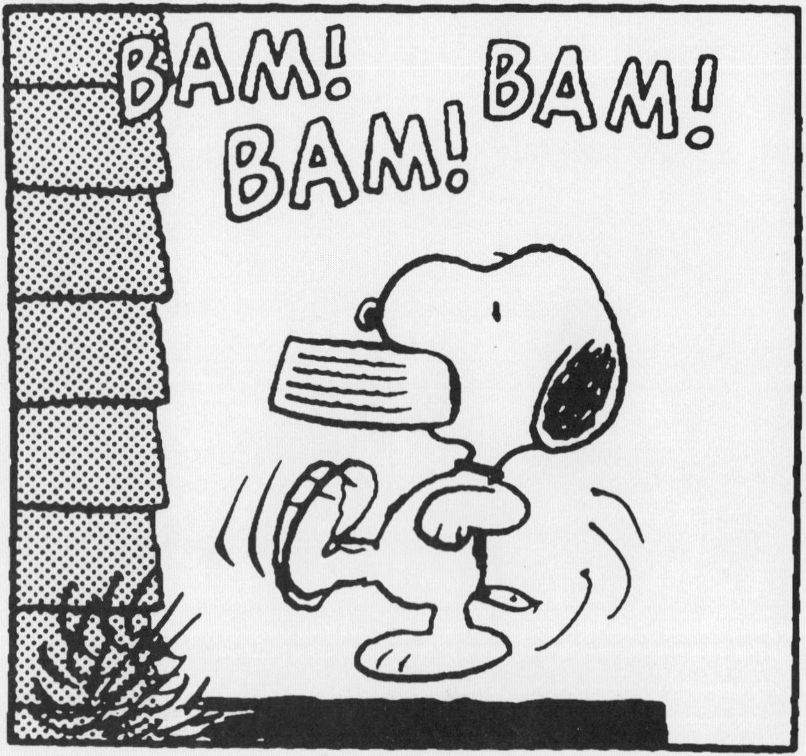
BAM!
BAM!
BAM!

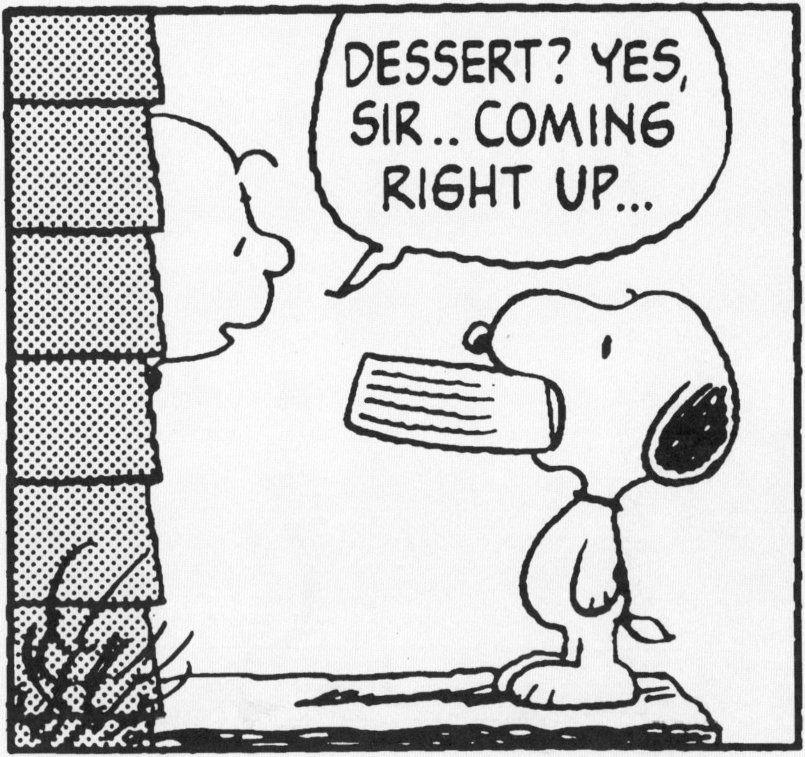
DESSERT? YES, SIR.. COMING RIGHT UP...

"THANKSGIVING DINNER"

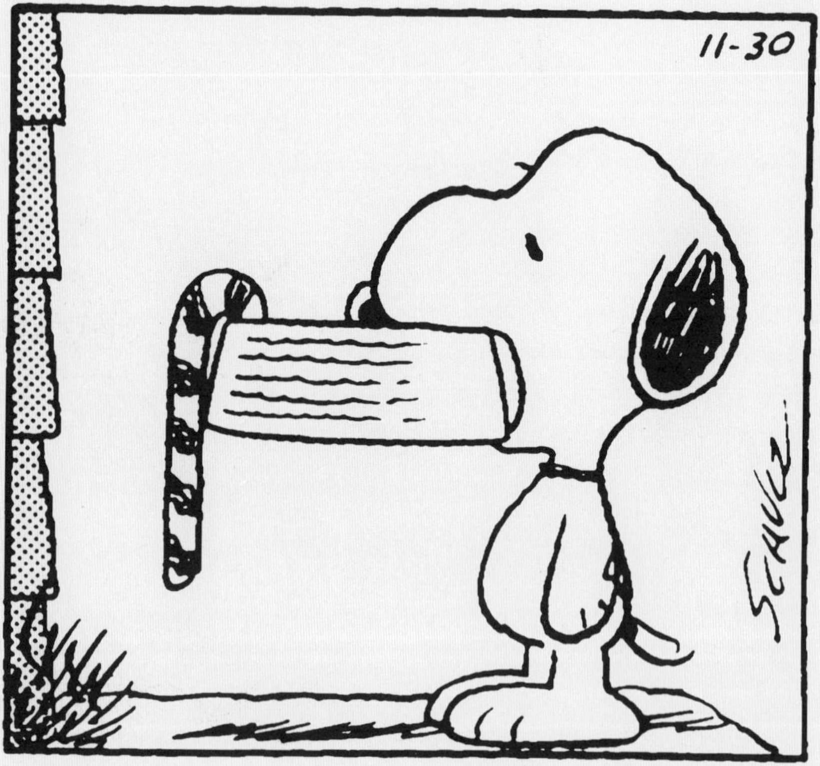
11-30
SCHULZ

"THANKSGIVING DINNER"

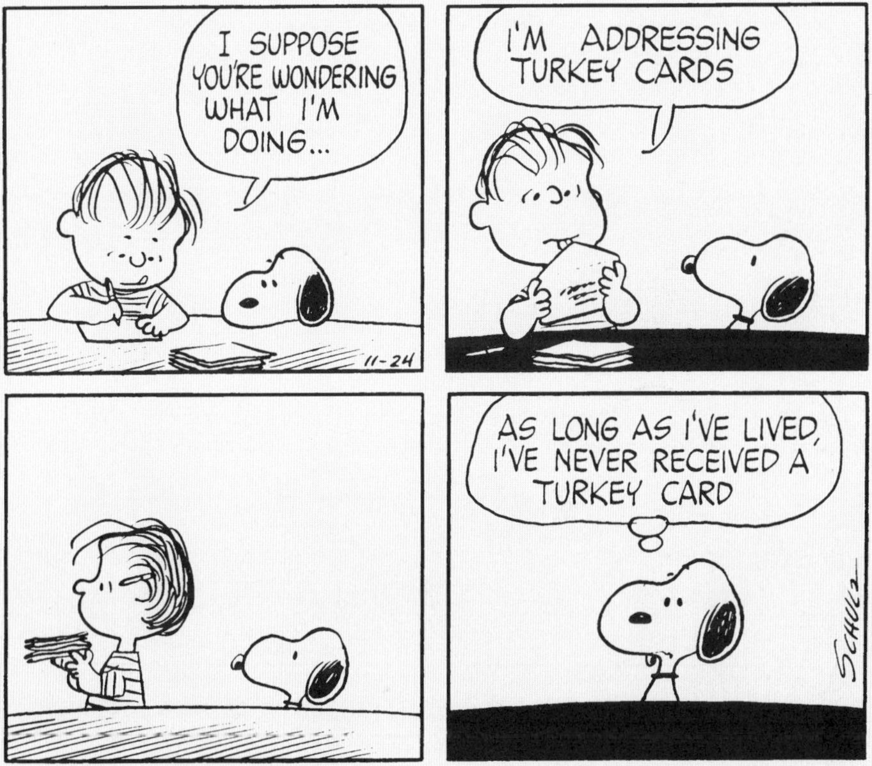
I SUPPOSE YOU'RE WONDERING WHAT I'M DOING...
11-24
I'M ADDRESSING TURKEY CARDS
AS LONG AS I'VE LIVED, I'VE NEVER RECEIVED A TURKEY CARD
SCHULZ

"TURKEY CARDS"

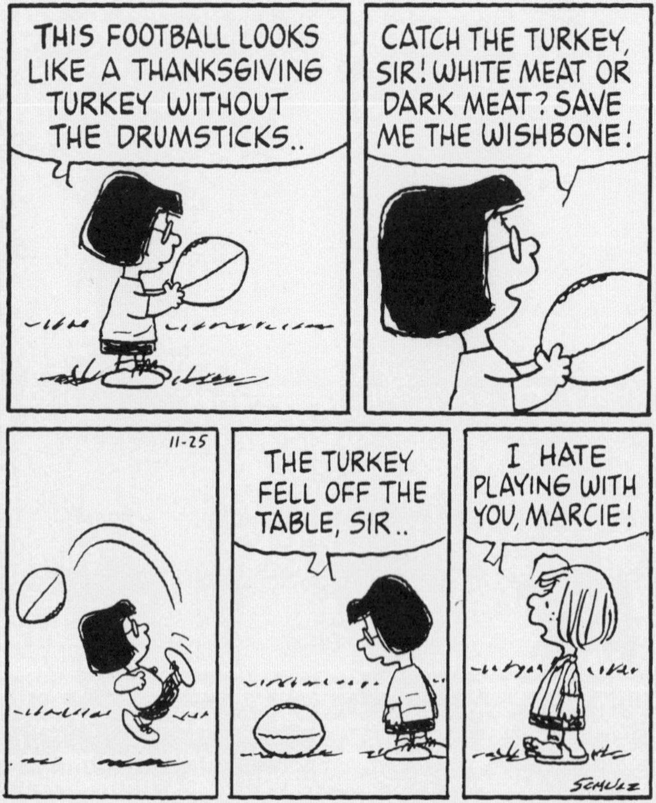
THIS FOOTBALL LOOKS LIKE A THANKSGIVING TURKEY WITHOUT THE DRUMSTICKS..
CATCH THE TURKEY, SIR! WHITE MEAT OR DARK MEAT? SAVE ME THE WISHBONE!
11-25
THE TURKEY FELL OFF THE TABLE, SIR..
I HATE PLAYING WITH YOU, MARCIE!
SCHULZ

"CATCH THE TURKEY"

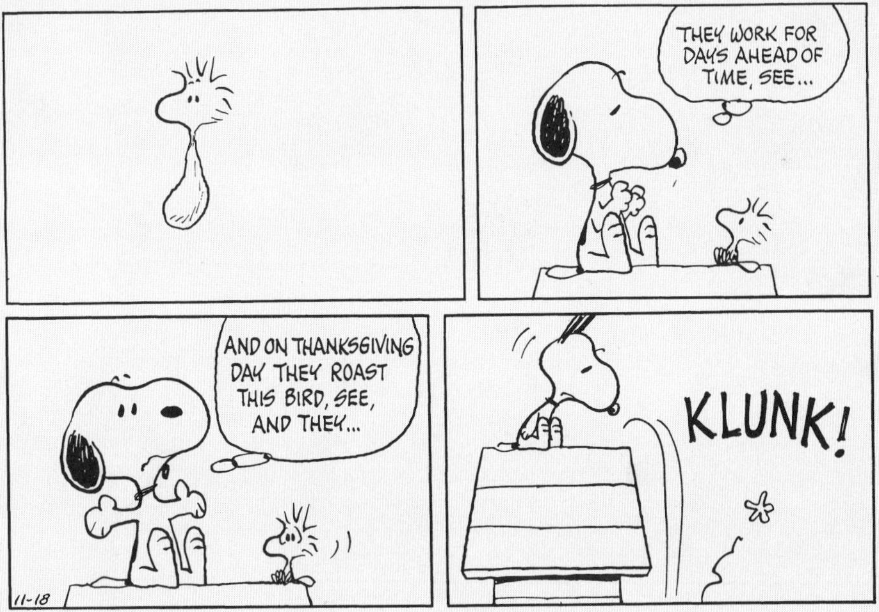
THEY WORK FOR DAYS AHEAD OF TIME, SEE...
AND ON THANKSGIVING DAY THEY ROAST THIS BIRD, SEE, AND THEY...
11-18
KLUNK!

"SAVING WOODSTOCK"

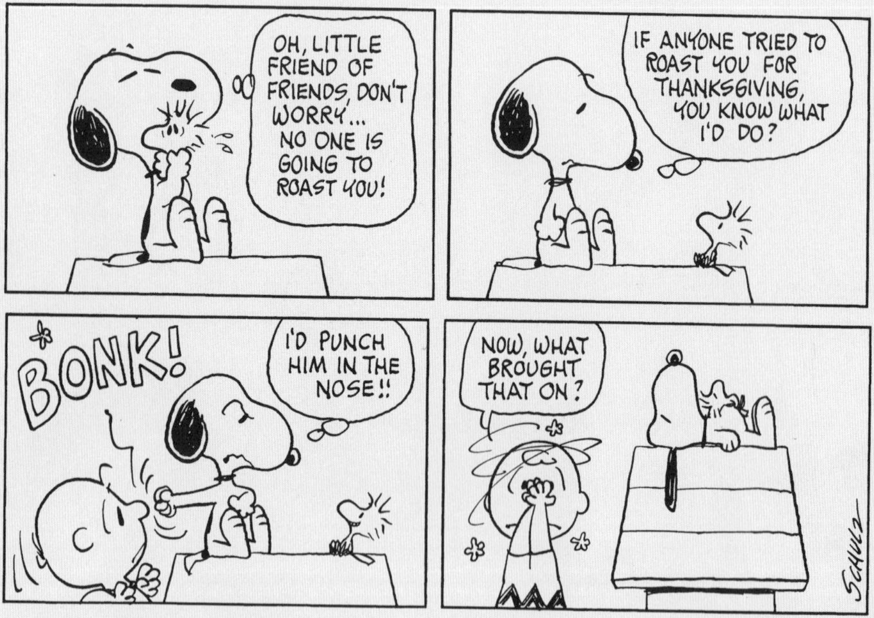
OH, LITTLE FRIEND OF FRIENDS, DON'T WORRY... NO ONE IS GOING TO ROAST YOU!
IF ANYONE TRIED TO ROAST YOU FOR THANKSGIVING, YOU KNOW WHAT I'D DO?
BONK!
I'D PUNCH HIM IN THE NOSE!!
NOW, WHAT BROUGHT THAT ON?
SCHULZ

"SAVING WOODSTOCK"

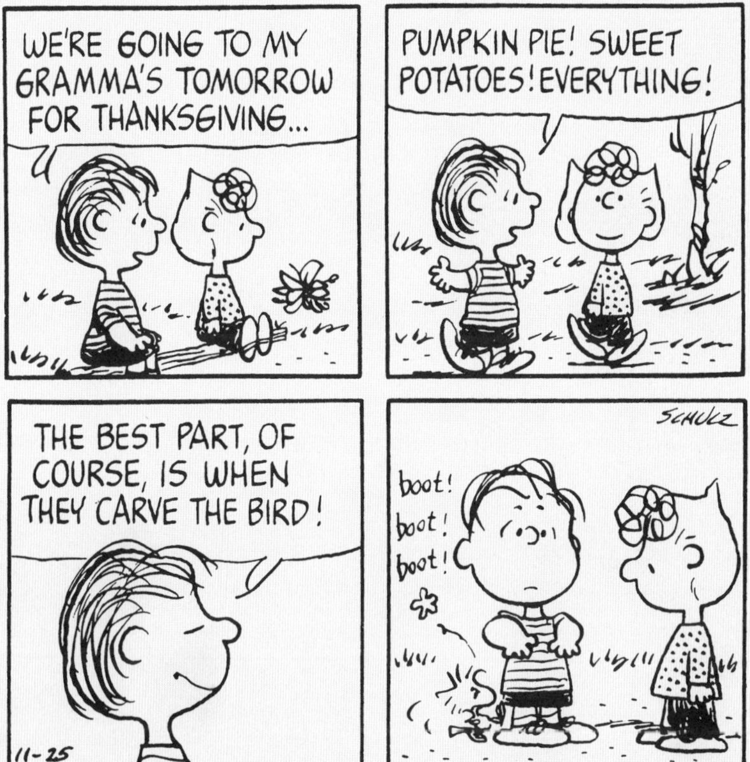
WE'RE GOING TO MY GRAMMA'S TOMORROW FOR THANKSGIVING...
PUMPKIN PIE! SWEET POTATOES! EVERYTHING!
THE BEST PART, OF COURSE, IS WHEN THEY CARVE THE BIRD!
11-25
SCHULZ
boot!
boot!
boot!

"SAVING WOODSTOCK"

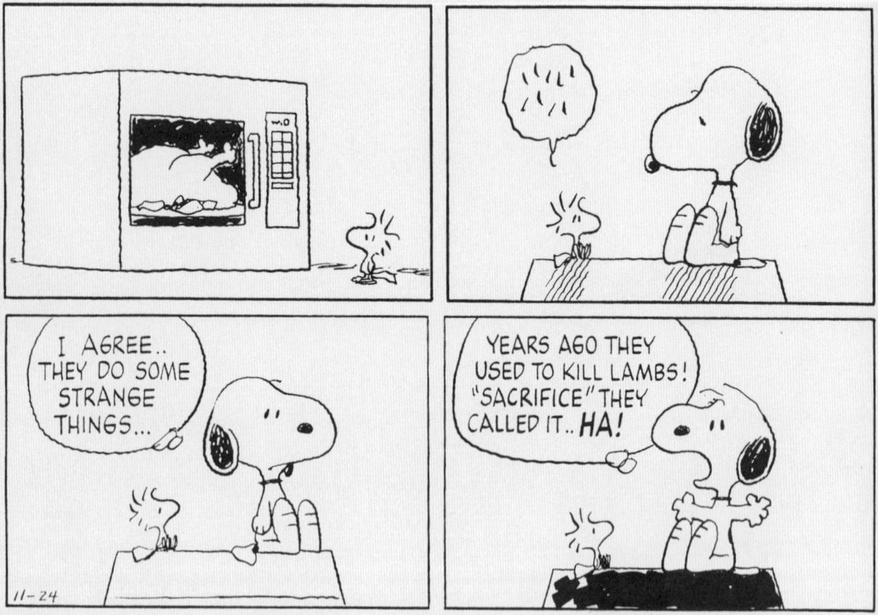
I AGREE..
THEY DO SOME STRANGE THINGS...
YEARS AGO THEY USED TO KILL LAMBS! "SACRIFICE" THEY CALLED IT.. HA!
11-24

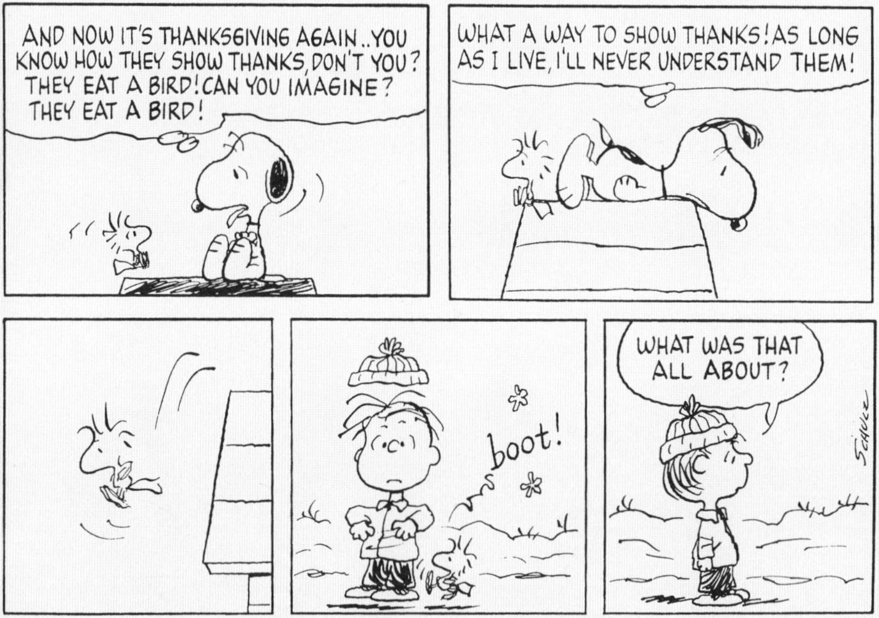
AND NOW IT'S THANKSGIVING AGAIN..YOU KNOW HOW THEY SHOW THANKS, DON'T YOU? THEY EAT A BIRD! CAN YOU IMAGINE? THEY EAT A BIRD!
WHAT A WAY TO SHOW THANKS! AS LONG AS I LIVE, I'LL NEVER UNDERSTAND THEM!
boot!
WHAT WAS THAT ALL ABOUT?
SCHULZ

"SAVING WOODSTOCK"

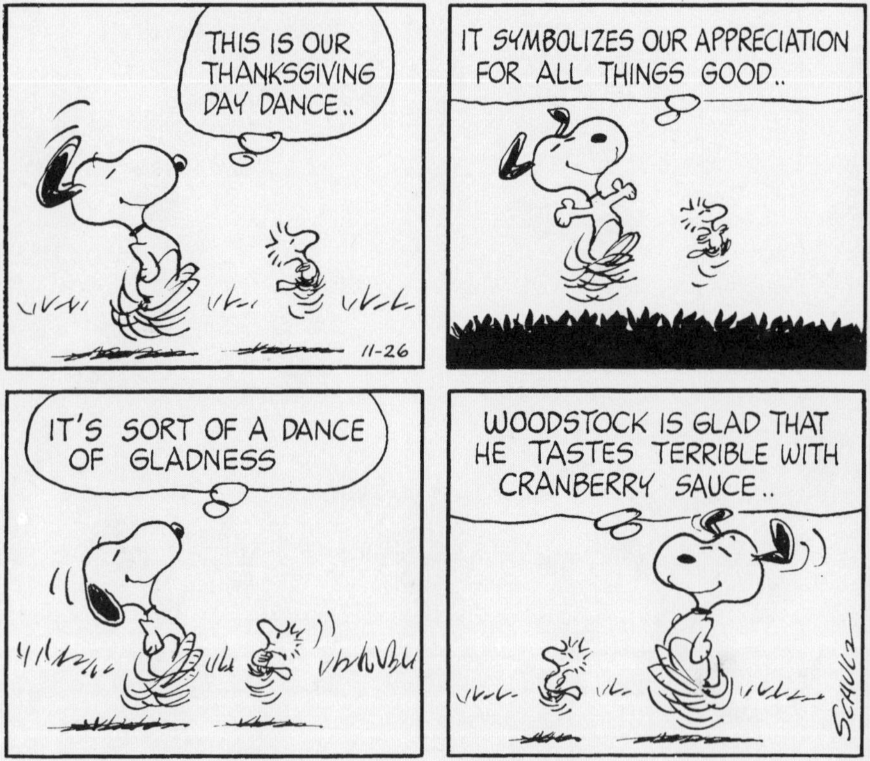
THIS IS OUR THANKSGIVING DAY DANCE..
11-26
IT SYMBOLIZES OUR APPRECIATION FOR ALL THINGS GOOD..
IT'S SORT OF A DANCE OF GLADNESS
WOODSTOCK IS GLAD THAT HE TASTES TERRIBLE WITH CRANBERRY SAUCE..
SCHULZ

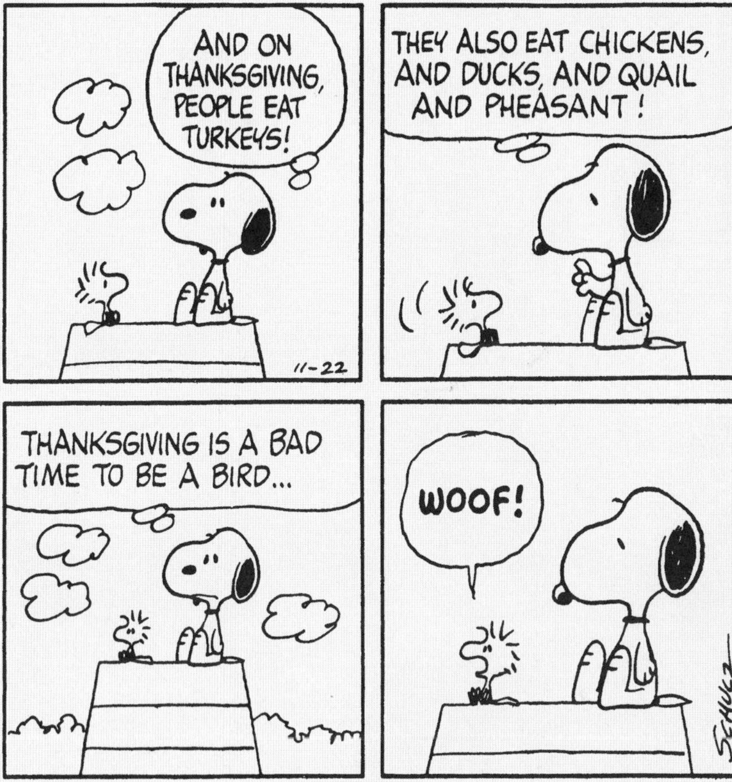
AND ON THANKSGIVING, PEOPLE EAT TURKEYS!
11-22
THEY ALSO EAT CHICKENS, AND DUCKS, AND QUAIL AND PHEASANT!
THANKSGIVING IS A BAD TIME TO BE A BIRD...
WOOF!
SCHULZ

"SAVING WOODSTOCK"

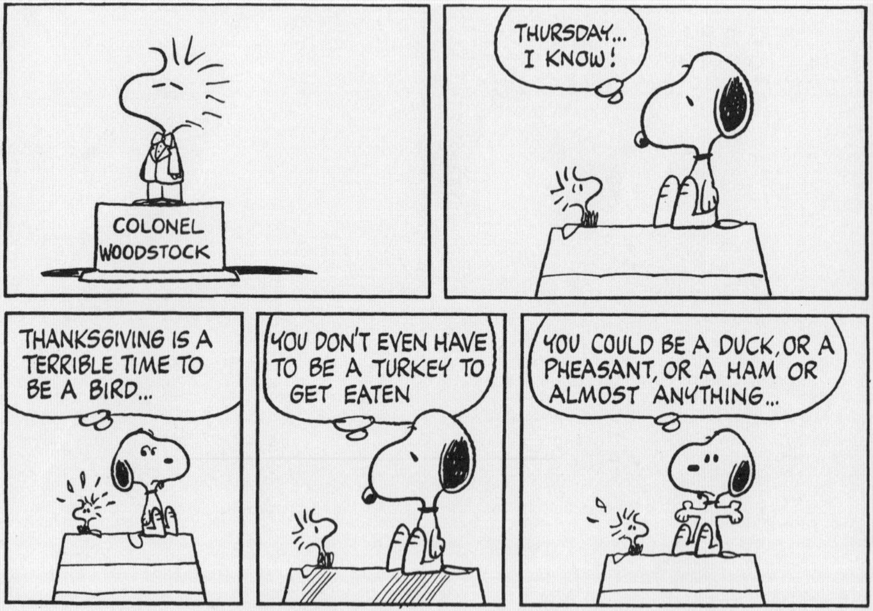
COLONEL
WOODSTOCK
THURSDAY... I KNOW!
THANKSGIVING IS A TERRIBLE TIME TO BE A BIRD...
YOU DON'T EVEN HAVE TO BE A TURKEY TO GET EATEN
YOU COULD BE A DUCK, OR A PHEASANT, OR A HAM OR ALMOST ANYTHING...

"SAVING WOODSTOCK"

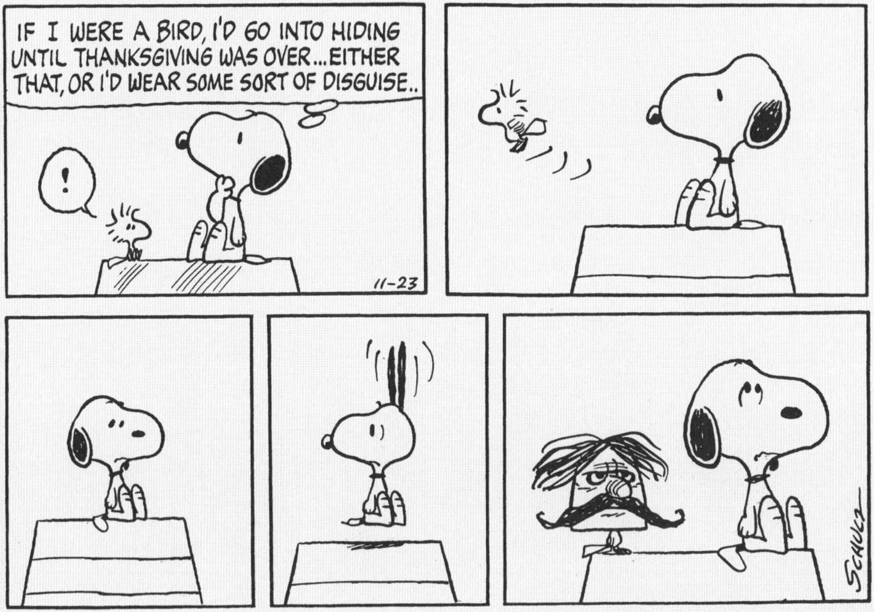
IF I WERE A BIRD, I'D GO INTO HIDING UNTIL THANKSGIVING WAS OVER...EITHER THAT, OR I'D WEAR SOME SORT OF DISGUISE..
!
11-23
SCHULZ

"SAVING WOODSTOCK"

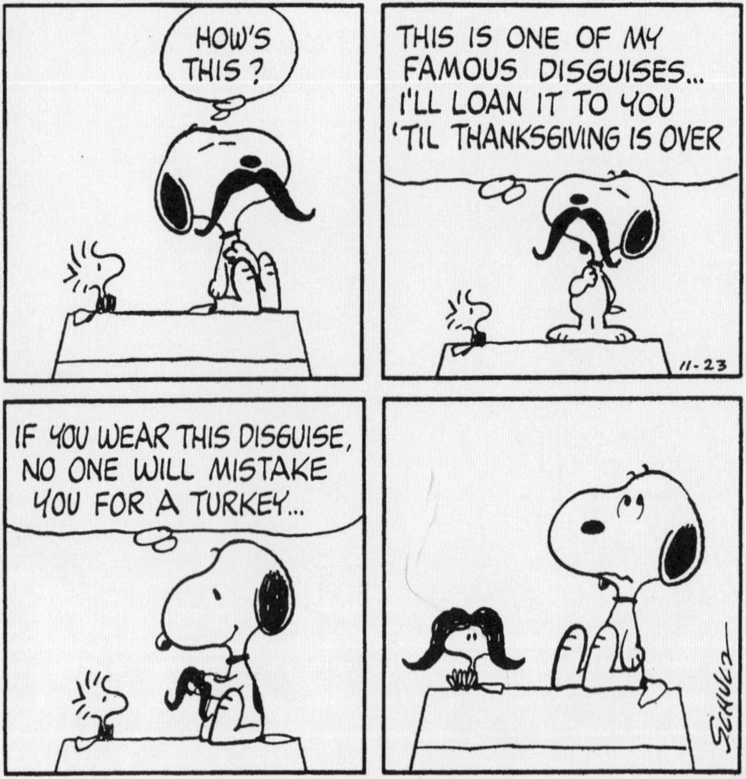
HOW'S THIS ?
THIS IS ONE OF MY FAMOUS DISGUISES... I'LL LOAN IT TO YOU 'TIL THANKSGIVING IS OVER
11-23
IF YOU WEAR THIS DISGUISE, NO ONE WILL MISTAKE YOU FOR A TURKEY...
SCHULZ

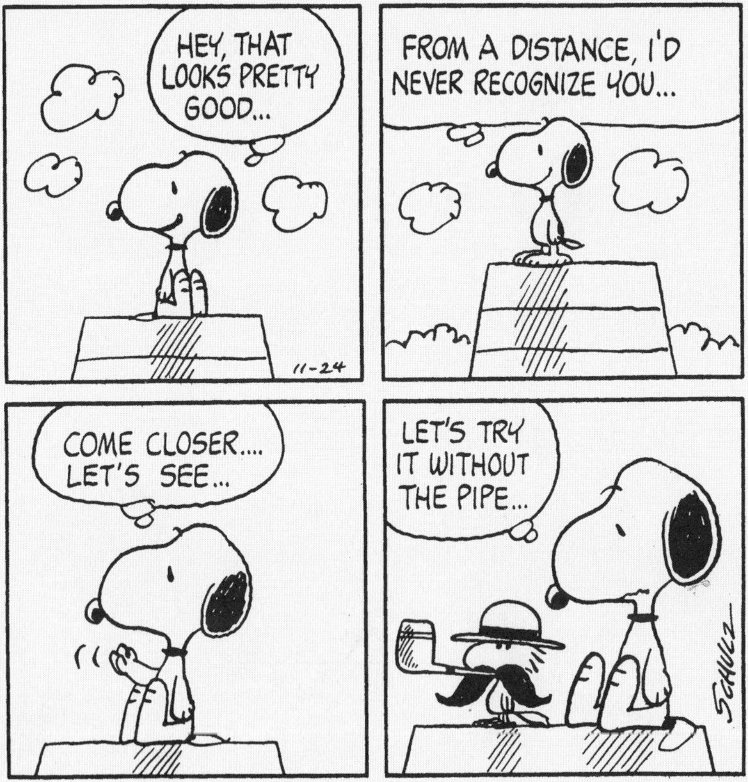
HEY, THAT LOOKS PRETTY GOOD...
11-24
FROM A DISTANCE, I'D NEVER RECOGNIZE YOU...
COME CLOSER.... LET'S SEE...
LET'S TRY IT WITHOUT THE PIPE...
SCHULZ

"SAVING WOODSTOCK"

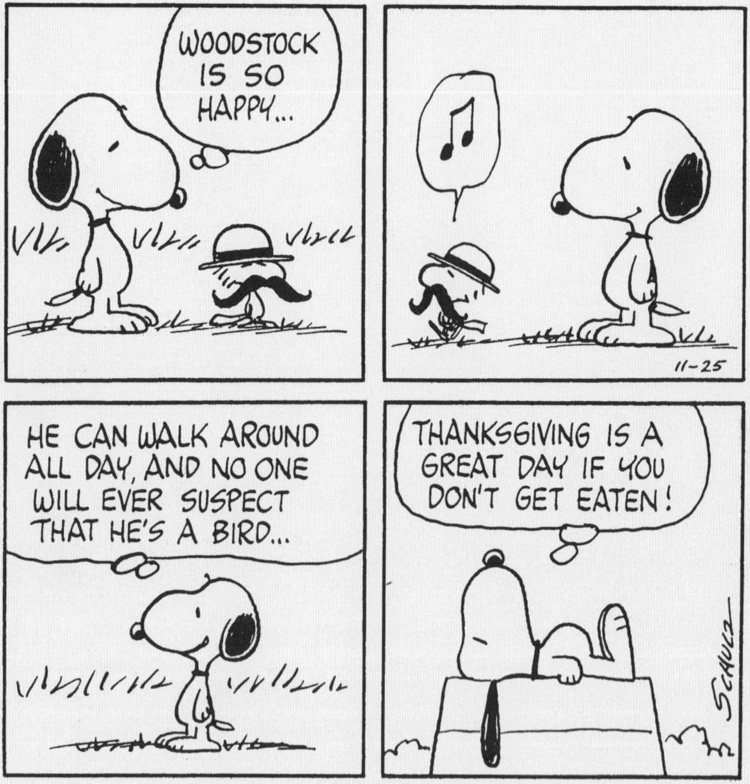
WOODSTOCK IS SO HAPPY...
11-25
HE CAN WALK AROUND ALL DAY, AND NO ONE WILL EVER SUSPECT THAT HE'S A BIRD...
THANKSGIVING IS A GREAT DAY IF YOU DON'T GET EATEN!
SCHULZ

"SAVING WOODSTOCK"

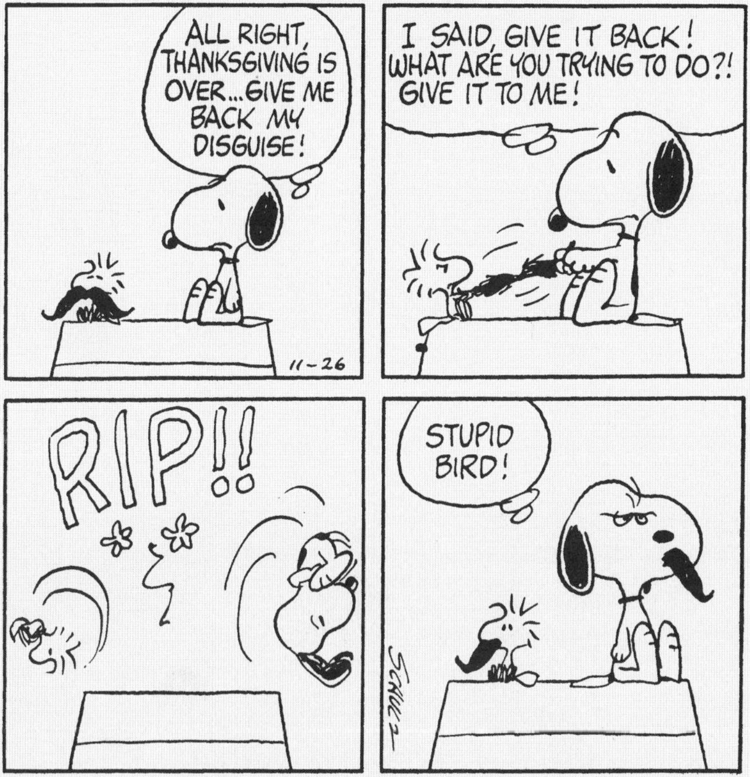
ALL RIGHT, THANKSGIVING IS OVER...GIVE ME BACK MY DISGUISE!
11-26
I SAID, GIVE IT BACK! WHAT ARE YOU TRYING TO DO?! GIVE IT TO ME!
RIP!!
STUPID BIRD!
SCHULZ

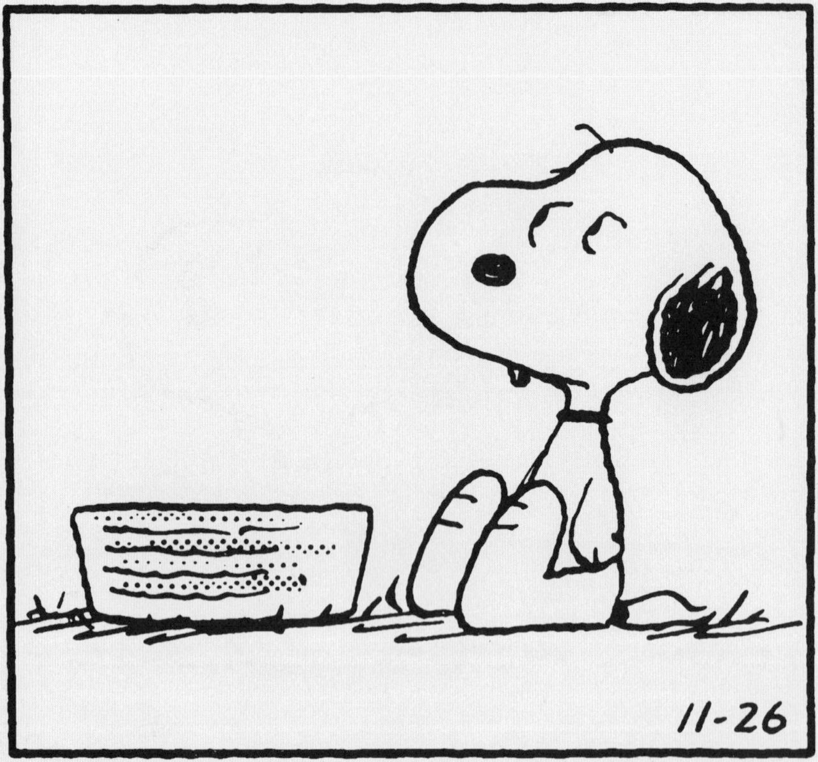
11-26

"SAVING WOODSTOCK"

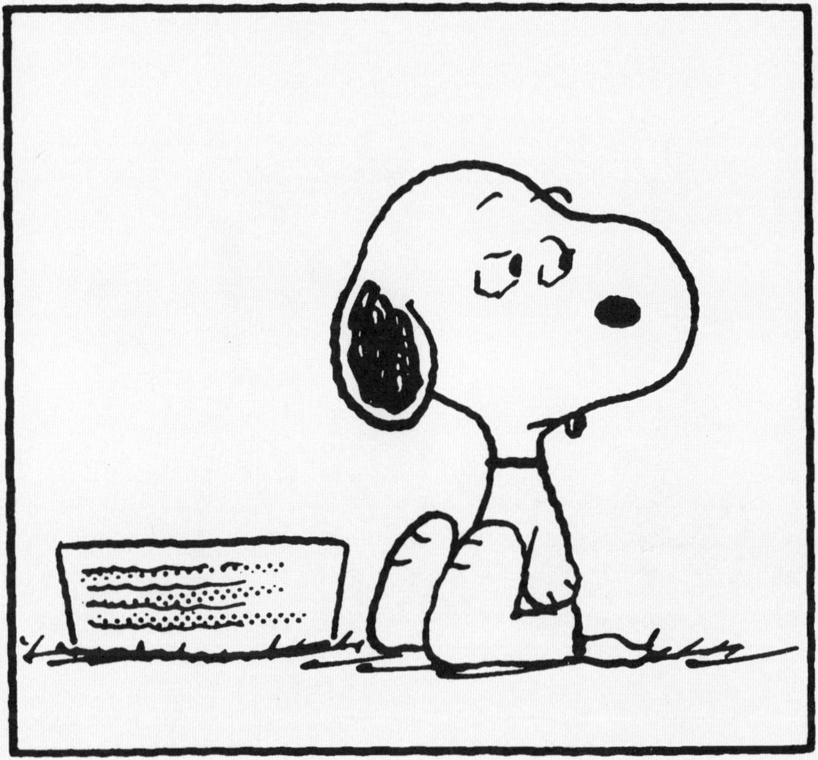

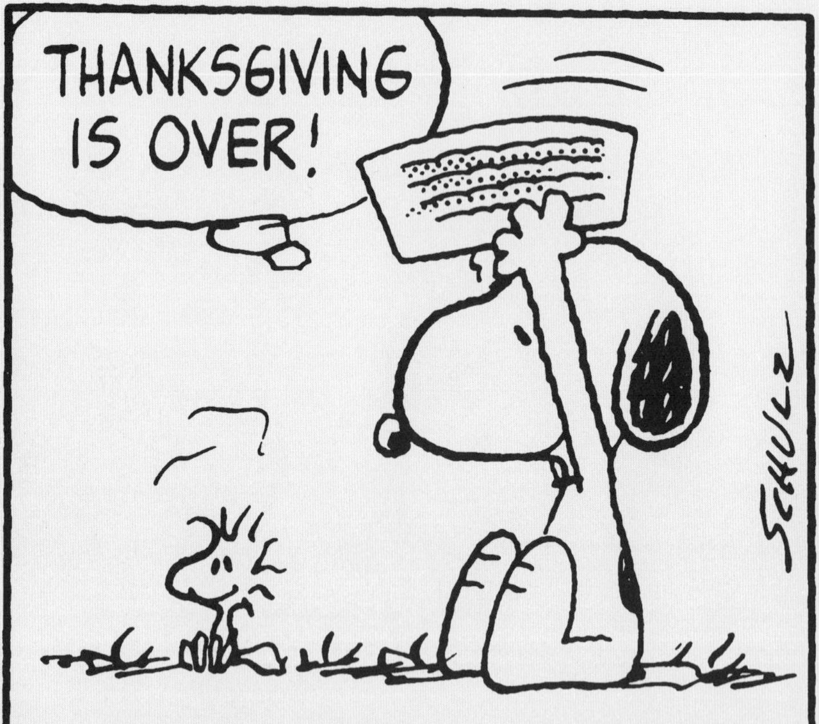
THANKSGIVING IS OVER!
SCHULZ

"SAVING WOODSTOCK"

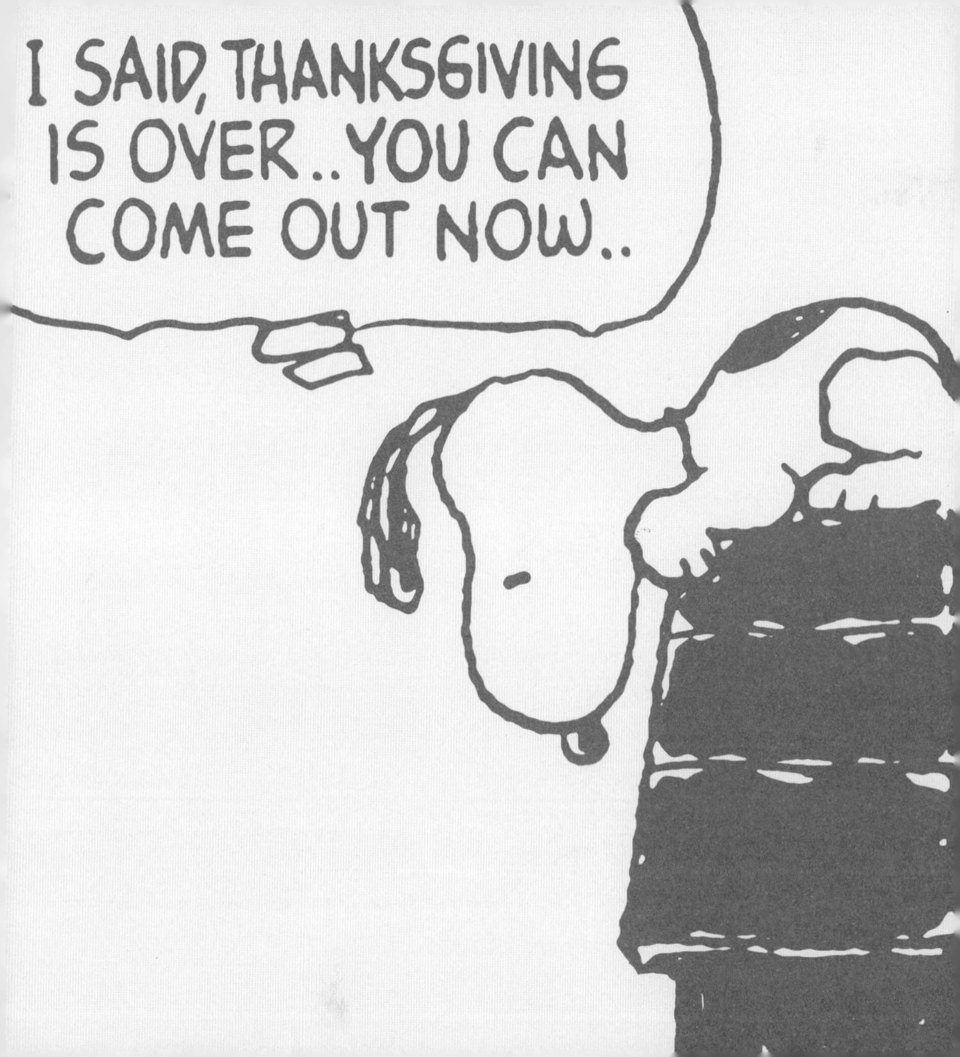
I SAID, THANKSGIVING IS OVER.. YOU CAN COME OUT NOW..

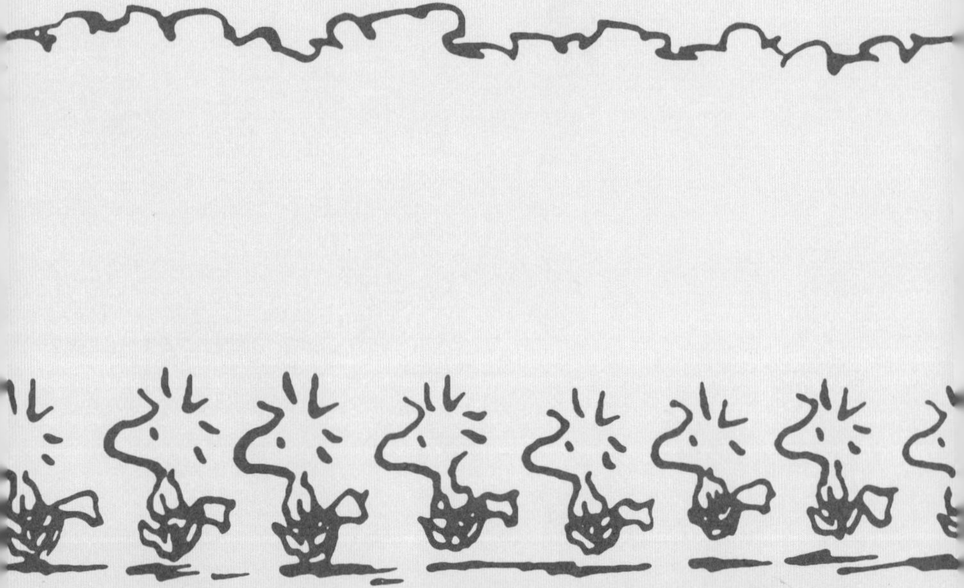

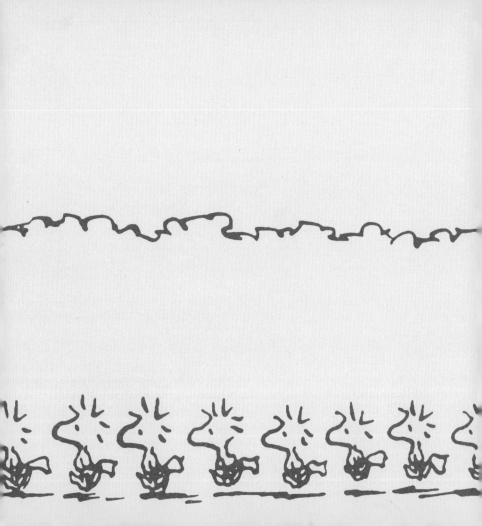

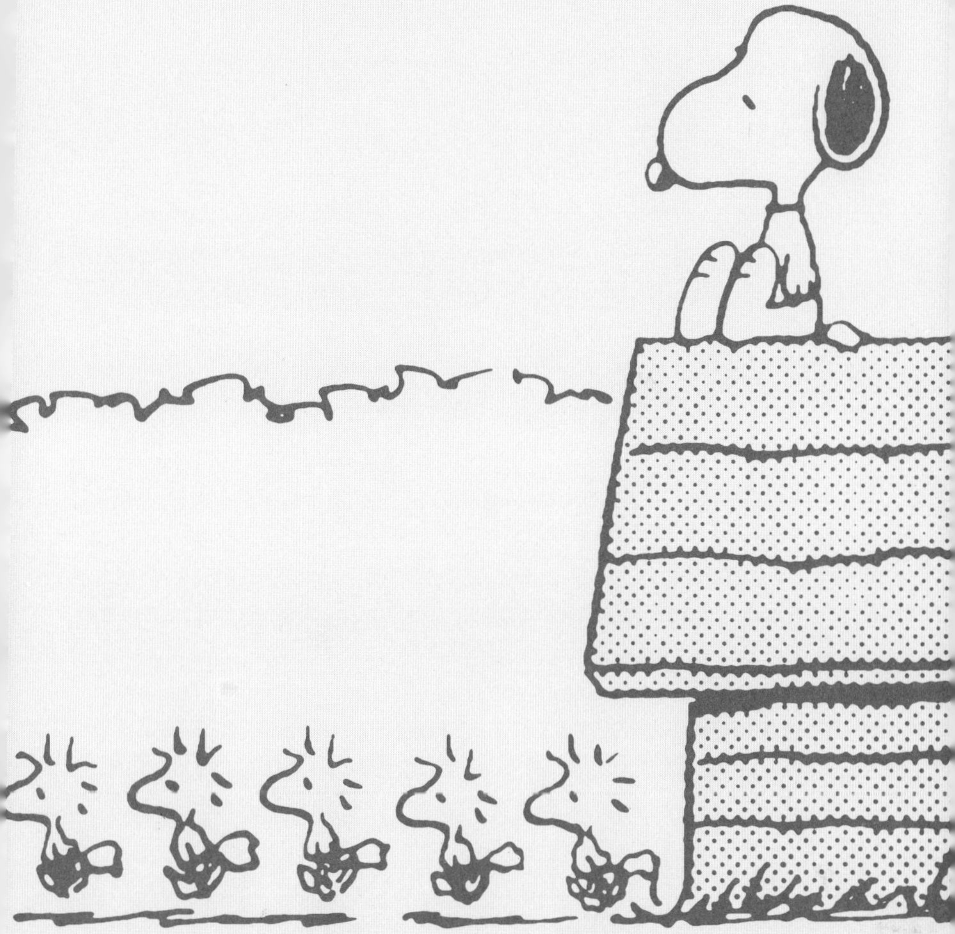

SNOOPY'S THANKSGIVING
Charles M. Schulz

Editor: Gary Groth
Designer: Jacob Covey
Associate Publisher: Eric Reynolds
Publisher: Gary Groth

Special thanks to Marcie Daniel for her invaluable assistance.

Fantagraphics Books, 7563 Lake City Way NE, Seattle, WA 98115, USA. For a free
full-color catalog of comics, call 1-800-657-1100. Our books may be viewed
and purchased on our website at www.fantagraphics.com.

ISBN 978-1-60699-778-9
First printing: September 2014
Printed in China

Thanks to: Randall Bethune, Big Planet Comics, Black Hook Press of Japan, Nick Capetillo, Kevin Czapiewski,
John DiBello, Juan Manuel Domínguez, Mathieu Doublet, Dan Evans III, Thomas Eykemans, Scott Fritsch-Hammes,
Coco and Eddie Gorodetsky, Karen Green, Ted Haycraft, Eduardo Takeo "Lizarkeo" Igarashi, Nevdon Jamgochian,
Andy Koopmans, Philip Nel, Vanessa Palacios, Kurt Sayenga, Anne Lise Rostgaard Schmidt, Christian Schremser,
Secret Headquarters, Paul van Dijken, Mungo van Krimpen-Hall, Jason Aaron Wong, and Thomas Zimmermann